FIGHT
SHIRLEY
CHISHOLM

by
JAMES HASKINS

Preface to the LibraryPress@UF Edition
KATHLEEN BENSON HASKINS

Introduction by Dr. Zinga A. Fraser

535 Library West
PO Box 117000
Gainesville, FL 32611-7000
go.ufl.edu/librarypress
librarypress@uflib.ufl.edu

Fighting Shirley Chisholm

Author: James Haskins
Preface: Kathleen Benson Haskins
Introduction: Zinga A. Fraser

Names: Haskins, James, author. | Haskins, Kathy, author of preface. | George A. Smathers Libraries, publisher.

Title: Fighting Shirley Chisholm / by James Haskins ; preface by Kathy Haskins.

Description: Gainesville, FL : Library Press @ UF, 2024 | Summary: Shirley Chisholm's dynamism, intellect, and devotion led her to become the first Black congresswoman and the first Black woman to run for the presidential nomination. In this carefully woven story, Jim Haskins tells Shirley Chisholm's story from childhood to her phenomenally positive impact for her communities and the world.

Identifiers: ISBN 9781944455309 (print)

Subjects: LCSH: Chisholm, Shirley, 1924-2005. | African American women legislators--Biography. | Women presidential candidates--United States--Biography. | Presidential candidates--United States--Biography

Classification: LCC E840.8.C48 H37 2024

CONTENTS

Publisher's Note..1

Acknowledgments...2

Preface

by Kathleen Benson Haskins...3

Introduction

by Dr. Zinga A. Fraser 7

Main Body

1. Early Years 11

2. Back to Brooklyn 28

3. Brooklyn College...53

4. Marriage, Career, and Local Politics.........................67

5. Assemblywoman Shirley Chisholm...........................89

6. Congresswoman Shirley Chisholm...........................117

7. Shirley Chisholm for President.................................135

8. The Fight Isn't Over Yet..160

Appendix..169

Bibliography..172

Index..175

PUBLISHER'S NOTE

Throughout his lifetime, Dr. James Haskins published over one hundred books for youth and adult audiences. Often coauthored with his spouse Kathy Haskins, these titles focused on topics ranging from biography to history, music to language, most centering the experiences and achievements of African Americans. The LibraryPress@UF is honored to present a new series of reissued works by Dr. Haskins that acknowledge his contributions as an author, scholar, and educator at the University of Florida while recontextualizing and enhancing his work for a new generation.

This series includes:
> *Fighting Shirley Chisholm (2024)*
> *Barbara Jordan (2024)*
> *The Cotton Club (2024)*
> *Scott Joplin: The Man Who Made Ragtime (2024)*

For each title, the LibraryPress@UF will produce an edition of the original text in eBook and PDF formats, with original or alternative images as allowed by copyright law and any prior agreements. Kathy Haskins has written a preface that accompanies each book in the series. Books in this series have been edited to reflect current practices on publishing hate speech and known slurs, where the first letter of the word is followed by asterisks. This allows us to ensure that the complicated history surrounding these words is not erased, but readers are not confronted with the full display of hate speech.

Beyond this series from the LibraryPress@UF, readers can access additional books by Dr. Haskins through the *Internet Archive*. We invite you to explore at https://archive.org.

ACKNOWLEDGMENTS

Of course, without the help of Congresswoman Shirley Chisholm herself this book could not have been written, and I am deeply grateful to her. Shirley Chisholm cares not only about racial minorities and women and the disillusioned and the poor in America, but also about America's young people. This is one reason why she chose to be a teacher, to work in the field of daycare. This is also why she consented to take the time to talk to me about her life, to read parts of the manuscript, and to supply pictures of her life. A simple "thank you" from me is not enough, but it is hoped that the thanks from the readers of this book will be—the thanks from young people for whom this story of Shirley Chisholm is intended.

Thanks also to Mary Ellen Arrington and Kathy Benson, who helped in the various stages of manuscript preparation.

Jim Haskins, 1975

SPECIAL THANKS TO

Introduction by Dr. Zinga A. Fraser

Editorial Liaisons: Perry Collins, Chelsea Johnston, Tracy MacKay-Ratliff, Valrie Minson, and Laurie Taylor

Design Editors: Tracy MacKay-Ratliff and Ella Terran

Production Editors: Katherine Nguyen and Cassidy Smith

PREFACE

Jim Haskins was born in 1941 in Demopolis, Alabama. He grew up in a working-class household with four brothers, two sisters, two cousins, and assorted other children whom his mother took in. "One of the places I found privacy was in books," he wrote in an author's statement for HarperCollins Publishers in the late 1990s. "I could be anywhere at all, but if I was reading a book, I was by myself." He concluded that statement with these words: "Books were once—and still are—a way to find my own private world. But they have also introduced me to a world far larger than I would otherwise have experienced. I love books, and I feel very fortunate to have been able to share this love with so many people."

Books were not easy to come by for a little Black boy in the segregated South. Jim's mother wanted to nurture his intellectual curiosity, so she acquired an encyclopedia set, one volume at a time, by purchasing certain dollar amounts of merchandise at the local grocery store. Black people were not allowed in the Demopolis Public Library, so his mother asked a white woman for whom she cleaned to borrow books on his behalf.

In 1979 I accompanied Jim to the Demopolis Public Library, where he presented copies of several of his books for young adults to the librarian on duty. "When I was growing up, I could not enter this library," he told her, to which she responded, "That was another time." We didn't realize until we turned to leave that Jim's niece was sitting at a desk over in the corner of the main reading room with her boyfriend. Another time indeed.

Jim was educated in segregated schools and later extolled his teachers for their missionary zeal in educating their students. He recalled that they displayed photographs of African American heroes throughout the schools (and took them down when expecting a visit from white school authorities) and tried to instill intellectual curiosity and love of learning in their young charges. He attended an HBCU as well as integrated colleges, majoring, serially, in history, psychology, and social psychology but ended up teaching special education in an elementary school in Harlem.

It was the 1960s, an era of movements—for Civil Rights and Free Speech and against the Vietnam War. A newshound since childhood, when he listened with fascination as his parents discussed the articles in the weekly *Pittsburgh Courier*, one of the leading Black newspapers in the country, Jim followed these movements avidly and discussed them in his classroom. He was eager to provide his students with reading material on their level about current events, but he was unable to find what he was looking for.

His first teaching experience impelled him to become a writer— almost simultaneously of books for adult and young adult audiences. His first book, *Diary of a Harlem Schoolteacher,* was published by Grove Press in 1969. It is regarded as a classic in literature on urban education and is still available in an edition published by the New Press. In 1970, his first books for young adults, *Resistance: Profiles in Nonviolence*, and *The War and the Protest: Vietnam*, were published by Doubleday. He later wrote biographies of African American sports, entertainment, and political figures, primarily for young adult audiences.

Jim taught as well as wrote for the rest of his life. After his first teaching job at the elementary school, he taught on the high school, community college, and four-year college levels— sometimes concurrently.

His writings indirectly led to his being offered a teaching position at the University of Florida. The Children's Literature Association was founded at the University of Connecticut in 1973 with a mission to elevate children's literature—then often called "kiddy lit"—as a field of study. Jim was invited to speak at the ChLA's first conference in March 1974, and he remained involved with the organization, developing an ever-expanding group of contacts, among them Dr. Joy Anderson, professor of English at the University of Florida. Dr. Anderson was influential in Jim's being hired by the University, and he joined the English Department faculty in the fall of 1977.

Coincidentally, at the same time, Dr. Anderson was spear-heading the effort of the University of Florida Libraries to acquire the Baldwin Library of Historical Children's Literature. Neither she nor Jim could possibly have foreseen that one day some of his books for children would become part of that collection.

There were few African American teachers at UF when Jim arrived. He always wore a jacket and tie and in downtown Gainesville was often mistaken for a preacher. When he explained that he was a teacher, he would be asked why he was downtown in the middle of the day. He taught Children's Literature and Adolescent Literature and, after he was awarded tenure, a course in Nobel and Pulitzer Prize-Winning Literature. He continued to write for children, young adults, and adults, and commuted between New York City and Gainesville until his untimely death in 2005 at the age of 63. Many of his books won awards, among them the Coretta Scott King Award, the Carter G. Woodson Award of the National Council for the Social Studies, and the Jane Addams Peace Award. In 1994 the *Washington Post* Children's Book Guild honored him for his body of work in nonfiction for young people.

In the year or two before he died, Jim arranged for a James Haskins Visiting Scholar Fellowship in African American Studies at UF. He also donated his professional papers and personal libraries to UF's George A. Smathers Libraries. He imagined the James Haskins Collection in African American Literature, which comprises both books he owned and books he wrote, serving as a testament to his wide-ranging interests and love of learning. He hoped that young people of color, especially, would be inspired to believe in their own promise. He would have been delighted that LibraryPress@UF has reissued some of his books to make them available to a new generation of readers.

Preface by Kathleen Benson Haskins, 2024.

INTRODUCTION

"Books were once—and still are—a way to find my own private world. But they have also introduced me to a world far larger than I would otherwise have experienced. I love books, and I feel very fortunate to have been able to share this love with so many people."[1] In that world Haskins opened up a world not only for himself but also to the many readers who were transported to places and times in Haskins's many books. James Haskins's biographies of African American athletes, entertainers, and political figures reflect his love for African American history and his commitment to preserving this history for generations to come.

James Haskins was one of the most prolific African American biographers, and he wrote a number of books aimed at young adult readers. Before conquering Shirley Chisholm's biography, Haskins would write a biography of Adam Clayton Powell and a comparative work on Black mayors- Carl Stokes, Richard Hatcher, Charles Evers, and Kenneth Gibson. Chisholm would be the first Black political woman that Haskins explored. He later profiled former congresswoman Barbara Jordan, who was the first African American voted into Congress from the South after Reconstruction, years after the release of *Fighting Shirley Chisholm*. Haskins published Chisholm's biography after she published her own two books, *Unbought and Unbossed* and *The Good Fight*. With much of her political life under public scrutiny, her autobiographies provided her the platform to craft her own narrative. Most importantly, Chisholm's books introduced her to a world who knew little about the first Black congresswoman from Brooklyn. Undeterred by the notion that everything to be explored from Chisholm's life would already

---

[1] Lionel Hampton, Hamp: An Autobiography by Lionel Hampton with James Haskins, (New York : Warner Books, 1989) ; Jim Haskins, "Autobiography." *Something About the Author*. Vol. 132 Detroit: Gale, 2002. 91-101.

be found in her own books, Haskins found a way to introduce Chisholm to a brand-new audience and discovered other entry points to her life. He was not interested in writing salacious biographies, as he often professed his disdain for writers who went looking for the "dirt" on their subjects; one could see his admiration for his subjects. Chisholm, who was private and guarded about her own life story, undoubtedly appreciated Haskins's approach, and provided him with pictures and items during his interviews that assisted in the drafting of the book.

As a former special education school teacher in Harlem, NY, Haskins undoubtedly felt connected to Shirley Chisholm, who was a former school administrator and devout educator. On an autograph given to Haskins, Chisholm wrote one of her mantras, "Aim High."[2] *Fighting Shirley Chisholm* provides a narrative to both young and old that many things can be accomplished when there is a standard of excellence. Chisholm's and Haskins's lives would reflect their journeys centered on achieving aspirational heights despite the myriad obstacles in their path.

Shirley Chisholm was one of the most dynamic political leaders in American history. In part, that dynamism was borne from her life story of resilience and her political boldness that continue to garner attention fifty-nine years after she entered public office. Yet, the most significant constituency of Chisholm's political life was comprised of young people. There is no other group that Chisholm spent more time speaking to than the younger generation. Whether it was interacting with elementary school children in Bedford Stuyvesant or serving as the commencement speaker at Howard University, Chisholm prioritized young people. During the late 1960s and early 1970s, she spoke to a generation coming of age during the Vietnam War and the civil rights and Black power movements, as well as a burgeoning women's movement. Chisholm would be confronted daily with

---

[2] Shirley A. Chisholm Inscribed ("Aim High!...") signed ("Congresswoman Chisholm"), March 8, 1973, Box 80, James Haskins papers, Special Arts and Area Collection, University of Florida. Accessed April 7, 2024 https://findingaids.uflib.ufl.edu/reposi-tories/2/archival_objects/265370.

young people who were wrestling with who they were and what they imagined their country to be during an intense moment of political, social, and economic unrest. The times also reflected a significant generational divide. Although depicted by some as merely an "old school teacher-turned-politician," Chisholm was beloved by a younger generation who did not scoff at her personal appearance and age and aligned with her fearless politics that rejected the political status quo. While a significant portion of political leadership was deaf to the cries and discord of the nation's youth, Chisholm not only heard them but she spoke directly to their concerns in her speeches and policies. As she told Howard University graduates, "You know that you must continue to fight the system that has been denying you the opportunity to be a total man or woman. But fight intelligently. Fight so that you get results and achieve something. You can't tear down everything and build everything new at once. Be practical. You can learn this from the men and women who have, in their own best consciences, fought the same fight before you, as they can learn many vital things from you."[3] Her connection to young people was not part of a political calculation to gain votes. Chisholm's speech identified both the frustration of youth who possibly saw destruction as the only viable option. Chisholm would affirm, her engagement with young people was not a political calculation. She declared, "Politicians tell me I'm wasting my time and energy. 'They don't vote,' I'm told. Well, I'm not looking for votes. If I were, I would get the same kind of reception that a lot of political figures get when they encounter younger people, and I would deserve it."[4] Unlike many of her peers Chisholm would be warmly received by thousands of young people all over the U.S. at talks and rallies.

Haskins titled his work after one of Chisholm's campaign mantras. Chisholm would often tour the streets of Brooklyn, saying

---

[3] Shirley Chisholm (NY), "Progress Through Understanding," Speech, *Congressional Record*, June 16, 1969, p.15972.
[4] Shirley Chisholm, "Youth and America's Future," an excerpt from *Unbought and Unbossed*. Shirley Chisholm, *Unbought and Unbossed*, (Boston: Houghton Mifflin Company, 1970).

"Hello, this is Fighting Shirley Chisholm."[5] In part, that slogan was Chisholm's effort to declare her autonomy as well as reject the gender norms that a Black woman was too weak and incapable of fighting for her constituents. Although by 1972, her run as the first African American and woman to make a serious bid for the U.S. presidency catapulted her to even more national recognition, the title *"Fighting Shirley Chisholm"* was not a rallying call of a political novice but a reaffirmation of her efforts to continue to fight for the most marginalized and vulnerable. *Fighting Shirley Chisholm* takes an honest look at Shirley Chisholm's career and life. As a Chisholm scholar and the historical consultant on the recent Netflix feature, *"Shirley"* I know that even more people would be drawn to Chisholm's story and begin to search for books and materials on her. Forty-nine years after Haskins published *Fighting Shirley Chisholm*, this books re-release should resonate with a generation that has experienced a Black president and an African American and South Asian woman as vice president. Although Chisholm's career laid the political framework for President Obama and Vice President Harris, her legacy of being the "Fighting Chisholm" on issues like a woman's right to choose, gender equity in government, prison reform, equitable funding for education, and increased living wages are as significant now as they were 50 years ago. The issues still exist and therefore Chisholm would undeniably proclaim to us that it is our responsibility to continue the fight!

Introduction by Dr. Zinga A. Fraser, an Assistant Professor in the Africana Studies and Women's and Gender Studies at Brooklyn College. Dr. Fraser is also the Director of the Shirley Chisholm Project on Brooklyn Women's Activism at Brooklyn College.

---

5 Shirley Chisholm, "This is Fighting Shirley," interview by Susan Brownmiller, *The New York Times*, April 13, 1969.

1.

EARLY YEARS

In the 1920s America was enjoying a period of unprecedented prosperity. World War I had created an industrial boom that was still going strong, even though the war was over. War matériel factories were rapidly being converted to peacetime production, and the atmosphere of hope throughout the country caused investors to pump millions more into new industries. The thousands of Blacks who had migrated from the South and immigrated from the British and French West Indies to work in the northern city war factories kept their jobs and wrote home to their relatives that there were many jobs yet to be filled.

To those who lived in the West Indies, the group of islands that lay like stepping stones between Florida and South America, this was indeed good news, for it promised a chance for escape from their own poverty and helplessness. Crop failures on the islands were causing famines; surely there was hope for a secure future in the United States. The West Indians came in great numbers in the early 1920s, traveling from the sunlit, poverty-stricken lands to the sunless concrete cities, settling near relatives and friends they had known on the islands. Like their friends and relatives before them, they came mostly to New York City, where the shipping lines had their terminus. There they swelled the already established island enclaves in different parts of the city. The Haitians favored Manhattan, the Trinidadians were predominant in Queens, and the Barbadians joined their fellow islanders in Brooklyn.

Charles St. Hill had actually been born in British Guiana, but he had grown up in Barbados, and thus he headed for Brooklyn when he arrived in New York unskilled, but full of hope for a better life. He quickly joined the clubs and mutual-help societies that flourished among the Barbadian population as they did among all immigrant groups. It was through one of these clubs that he was reintroduced to Ruby Seale, who was also a recent arrival from Barbados. They had known each other slightly on the island. Charles was older than Ruby, and in her early teens she was too young to have attracted him. She was still a teenager when she arrived in Brooklyn, but she had matured, and Charles St. Hill was immediately drawn to her. He courted her in the strict, proper manner insisted upon by Barbadians even in America, and eventually they were married.

Ruby and Charles St. Hill shared with their fellow Barbadians two goals in life: to own a house and to provide a good education for their children. To achieve these goals they were willing to work for the rest of their lives and to forgo many pleasures. The other West Indian immigrants shared a similar philosophy, for all had been reared in a strict, European culture, where ambition, thrift, and morality were stressed. As a group, West Indians were much distrusted and disliked by American-born Blacks, who called them "pushy," "crafty," "clannish," "the Jews of the race." When a West Indian "got ten cents above a beggar," a common American Black saying ran, "he opened a business." Among West Indians the group regarded as most ambitious and pushy was the Barbadians. In other words, while buying a house and ensuring their children's education was the goal of all West Indians, for Barbadians it was an obsession.

To the newly married Charles and Ruby St. Hill that goal must have seemed a very long way off. Whereas America as a whole was enjoying an era of unprecedented prosperity, many individuals in America were not. Although unskilled, Charles had expected to find a job in a factory, where much unskilled labor was needed. He was unable to find a factory job, however, and had been forced to settle for a job as a baker's helper. Ruby was an excellent seamstress and could perhaps have found work in a textile factory, but soon she became pregnant and did not go out to work. She contributed to the household income by taking in sewing. Their first child, Shirley Ann, was born in 1924. The next year Odessa followed, and two years later their third daughter, Muriel, was born. Charles found it difficult even to provide food and shelter for his family. Educating his daughters or buying a house seemed an impossible dream.

The 1940 Census record, which includes all six members of the St. Hill family. Shirley was fifteen. *Courtesy of Ancestry.com.*

Ruby St. Hill, a tiny woman and still very young, had her own difficulties taking care of three small children. Muriel, an infant, needed constant attention. Odessa at age two was hardly more than a baby herself and, jealous of the attention Muriel received, demanded equal attention. Three-year-old Shirley should have presented the least problem, but she managed, at times, to be the greatest.

Shirley was a precocious child who learned to walk, and thus to get into mischief, very early. Playing with her mother's sewing machine was one of her favorite amusements. "It fascinated me," Shirley recalls. "I would go to it and turn and turn its wheels. When mother went out, she tried to put the machine up where I couldn't reach it, but I piled up chairs and climbed until I could." Shirley was a tiny, wiry little thing, always active, always climbing up on or crawling under something. Her father laughingly called her his little bundle of energy. Her mother complained that she could not let Shirley out of her sight for a minute.

Shirley also learned to talk very early. The St. Hill household was a vocal one. Charles St. Hill loved to talk; when he arrived home from work he spoke in great detail of the day's events or of the latest news. He encouraged Shirley to talk from the moment she uttered her first word. He would sit her on his knee and pretend to carry on a conversation with her, while she babbled away in babytalk. By the time she was three she was lecturing her younger sisters and ordering them around. She recalls, "Mother always said that even when I was three, I used to get the six- and seven-year-old kids on the block and punch them and say, 'Listen to me.'" "My mouth," as Shirley refers to her talking ability, was to become famous.

Another quality that was to become well known was her strong sense of independence. Climbing up on chairs to reach a forbidden object was an early example. Being the eldest child helped. She had two younger sisters to whom she could feel superior. Being a child in a poor family also encouraged this independence because poor children are generally given responsibility very young. Shirley felt quite capable of doing many things that were beyond her mere three years.

Once, when she was not quite three, her mother had to go out, and there was no one with whom she could leave the children. Having no other recourse, she was forced to rely upon Shirley. "Take care of Dess and Mu," she instructed her tiny daughter. Most three-year-olds would hardly understand the notion of responsibility. Shirley seems to have understood it only too well. If Mama was gone, then Shirley was supposed to be Mama. When five-month-old Muriel cried, Shirley picked her up to comfort her. Mrs. St. Hill returned to find Shirley walking up and down with the baby, nearly half her size, in her arms. Mrs. St. Hill wanted to scream, but she checked herself, realizing that she might frighten her daughter into dropping the baby. "First she took Muriel out of my arms," Shirley recalls. "Then she screamed at me." Of course Shirley Chisholm has only a few memories of those early years, but when she speaks of them she invariably mentions a feeling, vague in the mind of a three-year-old, or perhaps created by the comments of her parents in later years, that her mother was a little afraid of her.

Young Shirley Chisholm is held by her grandmother, Emmeline Seale, in 1925. *Courtesy of Brooklyn College Library Archives and Teachers College at Columbia University.*

It was almost impossible for Ruby St. Hill to take care of three active young girls and to do sewing to supplement her husband's meager income. She and Charles could barely make ends meet. Often she despaired that they would ever be able to save any money, and she began to suggest to her husband that they send the girls to live on her mother's farm in Barbados for a while. It would be just for a few years, she explained, until they could save enough money to make their dreams for the future possible. With the children gone, she would be able to do much more sewing. She would not have to worry about leaving them alone when she went to the Belmont Market to buy cloth or when she went to deliver a piece of work to a customer. On her mother's farm, the children would have room to run and play, and they would go to the strict British-style schools on the island, which she considered far superior to the New York City public schools. She agreed it would be hard to send their children away, but she felt it would be the best course. After much discussion Charles St. Hill agreed.

Early in 1928 Ruby St. Hill shepherded her three daughters, aged three, two, and eight months, plus ten trunks full of food, clothing, and other belongings, aboard the steamer *Vulcania* bound for Barbados, the West Indian island farthest from the United States mainland. For Shirley, who was old enough to understand changes in the family routine, the trip must have seemed a great adventure. Exploring the cabin, peeking at the other passengers, feeling the ship roll and pitch in the wintry Atlantic seas must have been the most exciting feeling imaginable—at first. But the trip took nine days—an eternity for a three-year-old. Soon she was constantly asking her mother, "Mama, how much longer? When will we be there?" The pitching and rolling of the ship lost their excitement. But when land was finally sighted, the sense of adventure began all over again.

Shirley held tightly to her mother as they debarked from the steamer into the bustling port area. The sun shone hot on their heads, and the blue water and green trees seemed to shimmer in its rays. All around was bewildering activity—people arriving and going ashore, luggage-laden carts lumbering by, men and boys vying with each other to carry baggage or to act as guides to visitors, merchants displaying wares on hastily assembled tables and racks, crates of squawking chickens and sun-ripened fruit, the shouts and the creaking of wheels and the blaring of steamship horns, running feet and fast-rolling carts stirring up the dusty road so that one's eyes watered and one's mouth tasted gritty. Shirley can still remember the long lines slowly moving past the customs inspection tables and the equally long lines of people waiting for health clearance. Muriel, tired and irritable, began to cry, and Ruby snapped at Shirley for pulling too hard on her skirt.

At last they boarded the creaky, dust-scarred bus, and while their mother passed around the fruit she had bought for their lunch, she excitedly began to point out landmarks along the road-places she had visited as a child, houses where distant relatives lived. One tiny village blended into another, with their rows of neat, small houses and the inevitable chickens and stray animals at which the bus honked and which scattered, squawking and bleating and barking, from the vehicle's path. The dust ballooned into the air and drifted through the open bus windows, making even the fruit taste sandy.

Suddenly Ruby became businesslike, clearing up the remnants of their lunch, wiping the baby's face, patting the older girls' hair. The bus stopped, she gathered her girls and the hand luggage, and with a certain amount of clamor they left the bus. There stood Grandmother, and Shirley would never forget that first sight of the woman who would raise her for the next six years. "Mrs. Emily Seale, a tall, gaunt, erect, Indian-looking woman with her hair knotted on her neck. I did not know it yet, but this stately woman with a stentorian voice was going to be one of the few persons whose authority I would never dare to defy, or even question." Perhaps Ruby St. Hill had a reason in addition to the economic one for taking Shirley to live with her grandmother. Perhaps Mrs. Seale could tame her independent eldest daughter as she had not been able to.

All were exhausted from the long journey, but they had to wait an hour for the truck to arrive with their trunks, and longer for Ruby to go through most of the trunks to find their night clothes. Then it was time for a light supper in the large kitchen of the many-roomed frame house and baths in the big iron tub in the backyard, filled with water from the nearby well. Finally, it was bedtime, and Shirley, who rarely went to bed without protest, gratefully settled into the soft pillows, barely feeling the kisses of her mother and grandmother or hearing the door as it closed, darkening the room. Suddenly she was wide awake—how strange were the night sounds in this place! The clucking of chickens, the bleating of sheep, the singing of crickets. The city child, accustomed to the lullaby of traffic, of voices on the night streets, and of blaring sirens, would take many nights to become accustomed to the alien night sounds of Barbados.

But the days were full of new discoveries and adventures. There were goats, chickens, ducks, pigs, sheep, and cows to learn about. There was the small garden in front of the house to explore, with its yams, cassava fruit, sweet potatoes, pumpkins, and breadfruit arranged in neat, green rows. There was the house with its nooks and crannies to search and its doors to bang as one ran in from and out to the yard, a wonder in itself for children raised in a confining city apartment. On Tuesdays and Saturdays they loved to stand at the edge of the road and watch the women and men go to market in a larger town several miles away. Shirley was especially impressed by the women, who walked miles in the hot sun carrying loads of produce weighing up to seventy-five pounds on trays balanced on their heads. She marveled at how straight and tall they were, just like her grandmother, and, though tiny, she learned to walk straight and to hold her head high, as if she were balancing a heavy tray upon it.

Ruby St. Hill stayed on the farm for six months so that her children would be accustomed to the place before she left them. But even when the six months were over, it was hard for her to go. There were many tears and many reassurances that the separation would not be long—two or three years at most, Ruby promised. Although the children did not want their mother to leave, they were too young to understand the meaning of the separation. It must have been very hard for Ruby to leave her daughters—it would have been almost impossible if she had known then that they would not be reunited for six years.

The children felt the absence of their mother deeply for several weeks, but there was much to fill the void. Mrs. Seale may have been strict but she was not unkind. She loved her grandchildren, and though the household was poor, it was filled with warmth and love. It was also filled with people. In addition to Mrs. Seale and Ruby's younger brother and sister, Lincoln and Myrtle, the three St. Hill girls and four other grandchildren all lived there. Ruby's older sister, Violet, was also married and living in the United States, and she and her husband had made the same decision as Ruby and Charles had. It was best to send the children to live with their grandmother until they could save enough to provide for their future in the States. Thus, altogether there were seven children on the farm, ranging from just over a year old to nine. They played together and they fought together. At first Shirley didn't like not being the eldest, and she tried to assert her superiority, even over the older cousins. Gradually she learned to get along with the others better and to share more, but she did not lose her independence. There were times when even the oldest cousin submitted to Shirley's wishes rather than face "her mouth." "Even as a child," Shirley admits, "I couldn't understand why most people couldn't think like I did."

When Shirley was four, she entered the village school. Actually there was no school building. School was held in the church. Seven classes were conducted in the same large room, separated by blackboards and the arrangement of benches. The few books were passed from student to student during reading time, and lessons were written on slates with slate pencils. The subjects were reading, writing, arithmetic, and history, which was mostly British history since Barbados was a British possession.

In every way the village school operated in the strict, traditional British style. The different classes into which the school was divided were called forms instead of grades. The school day was long, from eight to four. The backless, wooden benches were hard, but the child who failed to sit erect the whole day received a rap on his back with a stick. Lessons were learned by reciting aloud, and although the large room sounded, as Shirley recalls, like the Tower of Babel when all seven classes were reciting, the children were not supposed to lose their concentration. "Spare the rod and spoil the child" was the maxim that teachers on Barbados, who used the rod often, believed. And parents backed them up. Any child who reported to his parents that he had received a flogging at school received a second flogging at home. West Indians valued education highly, and those who migrated to the United States stressed education not simply because it was a means of getting ahead in a new land but also because it was their national tradition.

Shirley came under the rod her share of times, but she does not look back upon those experiences with disapproval or resentment. In fact, she is grateful to her parents for making it possible for her to receive her early education in such schools. The floggings taught her to pay attention and learn, she insists. The strict teaching helped her to learn to read and write before the age of five, and she is particularly grateful for that. Years later, when she became involved in day care and education for preschool children, she often cited her own early education to prove her points: "I know that eye muscles are not developed enough for reading or finger muscles are not developed enough for writing, and I say baloney. Because I learned to read when

I was three and a half and I learned to write when I was four." Aside from giving Shirley a head start over the other children in school, learning to read early introduced her at a very young age to the world of books. There was no electricity at the farm on Barbados, but on many evenings Shirley would sit close to a kerosene lamp and read until her grandmother shooed her off to bed. At school her hand was always the first to shoot up when the teacher asked for a volunteer to read a passage from the book. Proudly she would read the words. Her permanent teeth grew in with spaces between them, causing a noticeable lisp when she spoke, but Shirley was not embarrassed. She knew she could read as well as or better than anyone else in her form.

When school was over, there were many chores waiting to be done back at the farm. First the children had to change from their school clothes, which were given out clean on Monday and expected to stay that way until Friday. Then they had to draw bucket after bucket of water from the well and fill the large galvanized iron tank next to the house, where all the water was stored for cooking and drinking and washing. Next they fed the chickens and ducks, gathered eggs, and changed the straw bedding for the cattle and sheep. The sheep and goats had to be let out to graze, and because there were no fences, the animals had to be watched lest they wander into the road. They had to be brought in when it got dark. Then the children would wash and the entire family would sit down together at the table for dinner, where the conversation was always lively and where every member of the family was encouraged to contribute.

Life was full of family togetherness, especially on Sundays. On Sunday there was all-day togetherness, beginning early in the morning when the children hauled buckets of water to the big washtub in the backyard, and, two at a time, got a good scrubbing. After a big breakfast the Sunday clothes were issued, and, scrubbed and starched and walking stiffly in their tight shoes, the entire family—all ten of them—set off on the two-mile walk to the church. Granny Seale always took the lead, walking tall and straight, clutching her prayer book and nodding to the other families on their way to church. Shirley clutched her prayer book and nodded just as her grandmother did, but she had to look down more often so she wouldn't stumble on a rock and soil her Sunday shoes.

Standing on a hill, the church always looked exactly like a church on Sundays and not at all like a school. As its bell tolled, calling the faithful to worship, one after another the families quietly filed into the church and took their seats. When all were assembled the first long session of songs and prayers began. No child, no matter how young, was expected to fidget, for they were in the Lord's House. But Shirley and her sisters and cousins did fidget, and they always received stern looks.

When the session was over, all the families filed back down the hill to their homes for a big Sunday dinner. Then they trooped back to church for another session of songs and prayer. Often the family would return home again for a light supper and then go back to church once more. Sunday was the Lord's day on Barbados.

Like the other children, and like her mother and grandmother before her, Shirley developed a very strong religious sense. This was not just because they went to church so many hours on Sundays but because God was always a strongly felt presence in the Seale household. And the prayers at church were not only to be said on Sundays—they could be said any time. Like everything else on Barbados, the prayers were English, and there Shirley first learned a verse that she would repeat often in later life:

It isn't the things you talk about
No matter how fine and true;
It isn't the way you seem to live,
Nor even the things you do;
It isn't the creed you call your own,
Nor the mottoes on the walls;
The only thing that really counts
Is what's in your heart—that's all.

It isn't the many friends you make
It's only the friends you keep;
It isn't the YOU that people see
It's the real YOU down deep;
It isn't what people say you are
Just let them talk as they please
It's what you know you are inside
What counts is what God sees.

Shirley attributes much of her success in life to her deep faith, a faith first instilled in her on Barbados.

The days passed—busy, active days. They blended into months and the months into years. The years blended into one another as well. There were no winters to mark the cycle of the year, no time when overcoats and scarves and mittens had to be taken out to shield bodies against the cold. The children went barefoot all year round, all the years round—sun-drenched years full of the sameness of happiness and security. But within the sameness there were changes. Each time Shirley stood with her back flat against the kitchen door, the mark for her height was higher, as were the marks for her sisters. Each was developing a distinct personality. It might be argued that Shirley always had a distinct personality, but under the wise tutelage of Granny Seale it took on greater depth. "Granny gave me strength, dignity and love," Shirley recalls. "I learned from an early age that I was somebody.

I didn't need the Black revolution to teach me that."

In 1932 they moved to another farm in another village. Life went on much as before—school, chores, family life. No matter where one moved on Barbados, the Caribbean was always nearby, clear, blue, and sparkling. One of the children's favorite pastimes was going to the beach, where they stripped off their clothes and rolled in the sand and played in the water. Their other favorite amusement was going to the market on Saturdays, where there were endless carts and stalls to explore and where one could snatch an orange and run away, lightning fast, before the merchant noticed. The market near their new farm was much the same as the other, except that the merchants did not yet know them and thus it was easier, at least for a while, to steal something.

School was also the same. Shirley entered the fifth form in the new school. She was a very bright student, and although the teachers were not in the habit of praising their students, Shirley knew they were pleased with her work. There were other bright students in the school, of course, but Shirley had an advantage over most of them. After the sixth form, most of the students would go into an apprenticeship in a trade such as carpentry or shoemaking or go to work on the family farm. Although there were two colleges on the island, few would go to them. In order to go to college a student had to go to a private preparatory school, which cost money. College cost money too, and most families on Barbados simply could not afford it. Shirley was lucky. From the time she had been old enough to understand—even before—she had been told that she would go to college.

Meanwhile, back in Brooklyn, Charles and Ruby St. Hill had not been faring as well as they had hoped. In 1929 the stock market had crashed, bringing on the worst depression the country had ever known. Although Americans of all races and classes

A crowd gathers outside the Stock Exchange after the 1929 stock market crash. *Courtesy of Wikimedia Commons.*

suffered under the depression, unskilled Blacks suffered most. Charles was fortunate that he did not lose his job, but as prices rose they found it close to impossible to save any money. Their plans for the future had not taken into account the possibility of a depression. Another unplanned event had taken place as well—a fourth daughter, Selma, had been born, making it difficult once again for Ruby to work.

At first, like every other American, Charles and Ruby had hoped that the depression would not last long, but as the years wore on they realized they would have to alter their plans. By the end of 1933 they had decided that, despite the fact they hadn't saved as much as they had hoped, it was time to bring their three daughters home. They missed the children, whom they had not seen in nearly six years. Ruby especially missed them and could not bear to be separated from them any longer. She feared they were growing up without knowing their mother. And so early in 1934, Ruby St. Hill again boarded a steamer for Barbados, this time to bring her children home.

How joyful was the reunion! After all this time, Mama had come back for them, just as she had said she would. Shirley could not stop looking at her mother. In contrast to Granny Seale, Ruby St. Hill was tiny and young. Her black hair was pulled into a tight bun at the back of her neck and her black eyes sparkled with happiness. She was dressed more stylishly than any woman Shirley had ever seen, and she was so pretty. "My mother," Shirley said to herself over and over again. "My mother."

For her part, Ruby could not stop looking at her daughters. They had all grown so. Shirley was almost ten years old now, still tiny and still possessed of that look of independence she had had when she was three. Odessa was nearly nine, and Muriel, only an infant when her mother had last seen her, was almost seven. They were all healthy and robust, and they babbled excitedly about how well they were doing in school and about their life on the farm. They asked a thousand questions—how was Papa, how old was Selma, the sister they had never seen, what did she look like? When would they go home? Ruby St. Hill looked at her daughters and wished she could take them to a large, warm, comfortable house and a secure future, as she and her husband had planned. But she and her children had been separated too long; she wanted them with her no matter what.

Within a short time Ruby had packed her daughters' belongings and enough food for the journey in the trunks used six years before. But the other preparations for going to America were not as simple as packing. Ruby and her children had to make several trips to the capital, Bridgetown, before they were ready to go. Each child had to be examined by a doctor to make sure she was healthy and would not carry any diseases into the United States. Each child had to have a long set of reentry papers filled out. Even though this was a long and time-consuming process, it was much easier for the St. Hill girls than for other children on Barbados who wished to go to the United States. Shirley, Odessa, and Muriel had been born in the United States and thus were already United States citizens. The number of native-born West Indians allowed into the United States was very low, and immigration often took months, even years, to accomplish. Finally all the medical papers and reentry papers were completed, and the St. Hill girls were ready for their journey.

The bulging trunks were sent to Bridgetown by truck. Then Ruby St. Hill and the children boarded the bus to Bridgetown. Granny Seale, Uncle Lincoln, and Aunt Myrtle rode the bus with them, trying to make gay conversation. Shirley was so excited she could hardly keep still, but she sensed the strain the adults felt. Granny, especially, seemed to be laughing too much and too nervously. When they reached the pier where the big ship was docked, Granny stopped laughing and began to cry. Shirley and her sisters looked at their grandmother in amazement. "I'll never see you again," she wailed. "You will never be my children again!" Then the girls and their mother began to cry too. After many tearful goodbyes they set off for New York, which Shirley remembered only dimly and Odessa and Muriel not at all.

2.
BACK TO BROOKLYN

The journey home early in 1934 was more exciting to Shirley than the journey to Barbados had been six years before, for now she was old enough to understand its meaning. But beneath the excitement was apprehension—would her father like her, would the sister she had never seen be nice, would she be able to make friends, would she do well in school? As the days wore on, the increasing cold and the stormy winter Atlantic seemed to intensify her apprehensions. It was so cold, so frightening.

Once on land the screech of the subway train startled them, the rushing crowds caused them to cling closely to each other, the tall stone buildings seemed to block what little sun there was. The cold wind whipped about their thin legs as they walked the few blocks from the subway station to 110 Liberty Avenue in the Brownsville section of Brooklyn. It was all very strange and frightening. But then their mother unlocked a door in the dark hallway, and they tumbled into a brightly lit kitchen, warmed by a coal stove and by the joyous outpouring of love among the members of a family long separated. Charles St. Hill laughed loudly and opened his arms to receive his daughters. Selma smiled shyly from behind her father's legs. They were all together at last, and only now did they realize how much they had missed each other.

But the happiness of homecoming did not long overshadow the strangeness of the new place for the three girls. The cold bit at their faces, their hands, their legs, indoors as well as out. The apartment was a four-room "railroad flat," so called because the rooms were lined up like the cars on a train; you had to walk through one room to get to another. The kitchen was first, then a bedroom, then another bedroom, then the parlor. There was no hot water. The only heat came from the single coal stove in the kitchen, which was the warmest room. In winter no one used the parlor; the heat never reached that part of the apartment. The girls slept in the first bedroom, which shared some of the kitchen's warmth. Shirley recalls: "Some days when Mother went to Belmont Market we children used to stay in bed most of the day to keep warm. To this day, I'm still afraid of the cold."

There were other frightening things. One was the streets. Most Brownsville children Shirley's age were able to run errands to neighborhood stores for their mothers, but they had not spent six of their ten years in Barbados. To Shirley, all the streets looked the same, and when she did discover landmarks, they proved

Belmont Avenue pushcart market (Belmont Market) in Brownsville, Brooklyn, NY, 1939. Photograph by Alan Fisher. *Courtesy of the Library of Congress.*

to be transient ones. Every time she thought she had the route to a particular store memorized, one of her guide-post stores moved away! And the crowds terrified her—all those grown-ups hurrying this way and that. They blocked her path, seemed to threaten to step on her. At first she walked in the street to avoid them, but then her mother scolded her: "Shirley, you're going to get killed by those cars!"

She missed the freedom and the safety and the space of Barbados. The flat at 110 Liberty Avenue seemed small and confining, and one could not simply run outside in New York as one could in Barbados. Cars were a hazard and sometimes, her parents constantly cautioned the children, so were people. She was not to speak to strangers. On Barbados there had been few strangers, in Brooklyn there were many.

And then there was school, which in Brooklyn was not held in a church. Shirley was enrolled in Public School 84, a massive brick building on Glenmore Avenue. Accustomed as she was to a one-room school that served the children of an entire village, Shirley was awed to think that there were as many as eighty-four public schools and that all those schools served only the elementary school pupils of just one of the five boroughs of New York City. Large as it was, P.S. 84 was so overcrowded that the students had to attend on double sessions. Shirley and her sisters were assigned to the morning session, which seemed a short school day for children used to going to school from 8 A.M. to 4 P.M. But these surprises were nothing compared to the surprises they received when they were assigned to grades.

When Shirley left Barbados, she had just been promoted to the sixth form, and naturally she had expected to be put in the sixth grade in P.S. 84. But to her horror she was not put in sixth grade but in the third grade, with children two years younger than she was! Her Barbadian schooling had been perfectly adequate in reading and writing, but because it had been a British system it had concentrated upon British history and geography. Now she was back in America, and she knew almost nothing about American history and geography. Because of her ignorance of these subjects, Shirley was placed in the third grade, and she did not like that one bit. "I carried rubber bands in the pocket of my middy blouse and snapped them at the other children," Shirley remembers. "I became expert at making spitballs and flicking them when the teacher's back was turned." She was bored, having already learned most of the material taught in the third grade. She was angry and ashamed to be in a class with children two years younger. She was frustrated, and in taking out her frustration she became a discipline problem. She could very well have been "turned off" by school because of this experience. But luckily her third-grade teacher realized that she was a discipline problem only because she was bored and ashamed. The school arranged for her to have a private tutor, and in a year and a half she had not only caught up with her age-grade level but passed it. Never again would she be a discipline problem at school.

She was, however, something of a discipline problem at home. She was even more independent now than she had been at age three, when her mother had first despaired of her "contrariness." For six years she had regarded herself as the head of a family within a family. She would never have challenged the authority of her grandmother, but among the children she had frequently aligned herself and her sisters against their older cousins. In Brooklyn, she often disobeyed her mother, and she bullied her younger sisters. The one person she neither disobeyed nor tried to bully was her father.

When the family had been reunited, seeing her father again had been almost like meeting a stranger. While she was away, memories of her father had been much dimmer than those of her mother. Her ten-year-old view was much sharper—she idolized her father immediately. First, she idolized his looks. He was a handsome man, tall and thin, his bronze skin set off strikingly by his hair, which had turned completely white in his twenties. Later, she idolized his intelligence. He had only finished the fifth form in school, but he was more well-read than many college graduates. "Even during the depression, he always bought two or three newspapers a day," Shirley recalls. "Mother never understood his spending the money; she thought he could get all the news from one. Papa read everything within reach. If he saw a man passing out handbills, he would cross the street to get one and read it."

But reading everything he could get his hands on was not enough. He was equally as hungry for conversation. He would often bring friends home in the evening, and they would talk long into the night about politics, race relations, unions, world events. Most of these friends liked to have a drink and a smoke while conversing, and Charles St. Hill made sure they were always comfortable. Though he himself never drank or smoked, he hastened to assure them that they could smoke, and he always had a bottle of whiskey on hand. Ruby St. Hill understood this habit even less than she did her husband's buying two or three newspapers a day. She often complained that the whiskey was all her husband's friends came for and that he should not buy their conversation with whiskey. She also complained that the girls had to undress in the next room; somehow she did not feel that was proper.

Shirley was glad she and her sisters slept in the bedroom next to the kitchen, where her father and his friends so often talked late into the night. She would lie awake and listen to them, wondering at the things about which they talked and about which she knew little. They talked often of the islands from which they all had come. Although they had left the British West Indies to seek greater opportunity in America, they maintained a lively interest in the islands and their politics. To a man, they were against the British, who owned many territories in addition to the West Indies. They called the British "oppressors" and scorned the good works the British claimed to have done in the islands, pointing out the profits the British reaped from the natural resources of the land.

They also spoke frequently of a man born in the West Indies who had been the first to preach on those islands what we would call Black power today and who came to New York in 1916 to carry his message to Black Americans. He preached a strong racial consciousness, speaking against even light-skinned Blacks, and encouraged Black-run businesses. The ultimate goal he advocated was the return to Africa of Black Americans, and during the 1920s he amassed a strong following among American Blacks. But then he was arrested on charges of using the mails to defraud citizens (selling by mail stock in various Black businesses that he had begun, some of which had failed) and was deported back to Jamaica. His movement essentially died with his forced departure, but there remained many Blacks for whom his words and his memory continued to live. For men like Charles St. Hill, the feelings of pride and consciousness that Marcus Garvey had awakened remained strong, and they spoke of him as a modern messiah who had been sacrificed to the cause of Black pride and consciousness.

When they were not talking about the politics in the islands or about Marcus Garvey, they were discussing conditions of Black people in the United States. All knew enough by now to realize that life in the United States did not hold as much opportunity

Marcus Garvey, National Hero of Jamaica, full-length, seated at desk, 1924. *Courtesy of Wikimedia Commons* and the *George Grantham Bain Collection at the Library of Congress.*

as they had believed when they first arrived from the islands. The depression had hit them all, postponed their dreams. They knew that Blacks were last hired and first fired. They believed that Marcus Garvey had been deported not because of mail fraud but because he had started to build a powerful Black movement. They traded stories about indignities suffered at the hands of white men and agreed that only organized Black movements like the one Garvey had tried to build would achieve real power for Black people.

Charles St. Hill believed that trade unions were one answer. He belonged to the Confectionery and Bakers International Union, and he often spoke of the gains the union had been able to make through organized demands and resistance. "When he was elected a shop steward at the bakery," Shirley recalls, "you would have thought he had been made a king. He had to have his shoes shined and wear a tie when he went to union meetings. It was the first time in his life he had been given the recognition his talents deserved."

Of course Shirley did not understand this at the age of ten. She only understood that unions were good because her father supported them. In fact, there were many things her father and his friends talked about that she did not understand, but she tried to listen intently even though she was drowsy. She also tried to relate the things her father said at those times to the things he said to the family at dinner. She knew he simplified things for his children so that they would understand.

Dinner was always a very important family gathering, just as it had been on Barbados. When Charles St. Hill arrived home from work, he expected the table to be set, and he expected dinner to be ready as soon as he had washed up and changed his clothes. The family would sit down at the table together, and not a morsel of the meager meal was eaten until Papa had said the blessing. Then, as plates and bowls were passed, he would begin the dinner conversation, telling his wife about the events of his day, asking about hers. He would turn to the children next, asking each one in turn what she had learned in school that day. He was not asking simply for the sake of conversation—he expected answers. For him education was one of the most important things in life. Although he was not one to voice regrets, he often stated that if he could have had an education he would not have had to work as a baker's helper. And he constantly told his children, "You must make something of yourselves. You've got to go to school, and I'm not sending you to play either. Study and make something of yourselves. Remember, only the strong people survive in this world. God gave you a brain; use it."

Usually something one of his daughters said reminded Charles St. Hill of a favorite subject, like politics or labor unions. If nothing in the conversation sparked his interest, he spoke of the latest news in the papers. Inevitably there was a lecture, and the younger girls would fidget in their seats, wishing to be excused.

Ruby St. Hill and Odessa would listen politely, feigning interest. Only Shirley hung onto every word. She thought her father was the most brilliant man alive, and she savored his words as gospel, even though many of the things he talked about were beyond her experience.

Her father frequently spoke of prejudice, of how white men in America usually got the better jobs, of how a Black had to be twice as good as a white in whatever he did in order to succeed. "America's got a lot to learn," he often said. Shirley believed her father when he said there was racial prejudice, but she herself had not experienced any real prejudice in Brooklyn.

Their neighborhood was predominantly Jewish, and most of Shirley's and her sisters' playmates were white, but Shirley did not give much thought to this difference because it was rarely brought up or pointed out. The difference she remembers most vividly was not racial but religious. She recalls, "We had a wonderful time going out on the fire escape and watching the old Jewish rabbis standing around their synagogues on Saturdays and rocking back and forth. We didn't know it was the way they prayed, so we would imitate them and laugh at them." It also seemed very strange to the St. Hill girls that their Jewish playmates went to synagogue on Saturday. "You've got your days mixed up," they'd call out laughingly, as their friends passed. "You've got your days mixed up!" their friends would chide as the St. Hill girls set off for church. By Monday, both synagogue and church seemed far away, and the children, Jewish and Christian, played together happily.

A similar lack of racial tension existed between Ruby St. Hill and the Jewish women of the neighborhood. Differences were acknowledged, but more often than not in a joking way, as when Ruby imitated the heavy accents of the Jewish women. Many of them spoke and read English very poorly, and Ruby, with her excellent English, was often asked for help in explaining apartment leases and other legal contracts. As Shirley recalls, "She became a kind of neighborhood oracle and leader."

At school the racial situation was much the same as in the neighborhood. P.S. 84 was about 80 percent white and mostly Jewish. All the teachers were white, and most were also Jewish. This ratio was not particularly noticed by Shirley and her sisters. As Shirley recalls, "At that time the race line was not drawn in the same way it is today."

This is not to say that the St. Hill girls did not have racial consciousness. Indeed, their parents, especially their father, instilled in them a strong racial consciousness. But it was a positive, not a negative consciousness. The girls were brought up to feel pretty and bright and capable of success, as long as they worked hard for it. They were also brought up with a strong religious faith, a faith that would help them greatly in times of need in later life.

If Shirley, Odessa, and Muriel had thought that in moving to Brooklyn they would escape the all-day church sessions they had had to endure on Barbados, they were very wrong. The English Brethren Church, to which Mrs. St. Hill belonged, required its faithful to attend three separate services on Sunday. It had been established by West Indians, who felt that maintaining the old ways was more important than belonging to a church that had a minister. The English Brethren Church had no minister and no formal service, but its members conducted their own sessions of prayer and preaching. Shirley remembers that the neighborhood Jewish children got a great kick out of the idea that she and her sisters had to go to church so often on Sunday. "They would chant, 'Here come the St. Hill girls!' as Mother, Odessa, Muriel, Selma, and I, dressed up and each carrying a little Bible, walked to 11:00 A.M. service, 2:30 P.M. Bible service, and 7:30 P.M. service at the English Brethren Church."

But despite the long church sessions and the Sunday jeers of their playmates, life in Brooklyn was fairly happy for the three Barbados-raised children. Once they grew accustomed to the new ways and environment, they settled into their new life contentedly, and with each month that passed Barbados faded further into the backs of their minds, becoming, finally, a warm, sunny, happy dream. They were growing, and many other things filled their minds.

Aware that the girls were growing up, Ruby St. Hill decided the family needed a larger apartment. "Our daughters need more room," she told her husband. "We all need more room. Besides, they get too many colds every winter. We need a steam heated apartment." Mrs. St. Hill searched for weeks for another place. During the depression it was not hard to find apartments. Many were vacated by tenants who could no longer afford to pay the rent. What was hard for Mrs. St. Hill was finding an apartment her family could afford. Finally she found one at 420 Ralph Avenue in the Bedford-Stuyvesant section of Brooklyn. It had only four rooms, like the Liberty Avenue apartment, but it was bigger, roomier, and all the rooms were heated in winter, not just the kitchen. The rent was higher than that of the Brownsville flat, but Mrs. St. Hill had gone over the family budget and decided that if they cut a few corners on other things, they could afford it. Shortly after, they moved into the Ralph Avenue apartment.

Shirley liked the new apartment much better than the old. It was warmer, and even though it was still not big enough to ensure privacy, one could find a quiet corner in which to read or play. The neighborhood was another matter. Bedford-Stuyvesant was at this time about 50 percent Black, and the atmosphere of the community was typical of an area where one group is fighting to retain control while another group is steadily making inroads. The older, Jewish residents felt threatened by the influx of Blacks arriving mostly from the South. The Black newcomers responded to the Jewish hostility with hostility of their own. For the first time Shirley heard racial slurs like "n*****" and "kike." "N*****" was more often shouted publicly, "kike" was usually muttered. There was little concept of Black power among the residents, who tended to accept, at least outwardly, the discrimination they encountered. But it was hard for their children to accept. "The Jewish children would tell me their mothers had forbidden them to play with me," Shirley recalls. "I was not used to Black being used as a derogatory word."

Racial tension could also be felt at P.S. 28, where Shirley and her sisters were now enrolled. There were fights between Black and white students, and students grouped themselves according to race. While Shirley had hardly thought about the fact that all the teachers at P.S. 84 were white, at P.S. 28 she began to notice and to wonder if they would treat her fairly. "They'd better," she said to herself, "because I'm one of the smartest students in the class." Shirley did not experience any discrimination from her teachers. The results of tests had shown that her IQ was 170, at the near-genius level. In fact, she skipped to a higher grade and shortly entered Junior High School 178.

Meanwhile, Charles and Ruby St. Hill were finding it a struggle to remain in the new apartment. For a year or so they had tried to cut every corner they possibly could, and they still could not afford the rent. Mr. St. Hill had changed jobs, leaving the bakery to work in a factory that made burlap bags. He had expected to make several dollars a week more at the burlap factory, but the hardest years of the depression were upon America, and that factory, like many others, was unable to maintain a full production schedule. Charles St. Hill's work week was shortened, and then shortened again until sometimes he was working as little as two days a week and bringing home only eighteen dollars. This could hardly pay for the family's groceries, let alone the rent. At last it was decided that Mrs. St. Hill must go to work. Even if she sewed all day, she could not earn enough money at home.

Mrs. St. Hill got a job as a domestic, working for white families in the nearby Flatbush section of Brooklyn. She certainly could not afford to pay a baby-sitter, and so she had to do the one thing she had always hoped not to have to do. She put an apartment key on a string and hung it around Shirley's neck.

Shirley became what is known in poor city neighborhoods as a "latch-key child." Every school day at lunch time, she walked from J.H.S. 178 to P.S. 28 to pick up Odessa, Muriel, and Selma and then shepherded them home. When they reached the apartment, she carefully took the key and, without removing the string from around her neck, unlocked the door. Lunch was simple, usually just a bun and a glass of milk, but Shirley would set it out as carefully as if it were a full-course meal. Sitting at the head of the table, she would watch over her charges. "Hurry up, Selma, don't dawdle. We have to get back to school." The girls resented her superior manner: "You're bullying us, Shirley, we're going to tell Mama." "You're bullying us, Shirley," Shirley would mimic. There was no question in her mind that she was doing the right thing. When lunch was over, she carefully locked the door of the apartment, returned her sisters to P.S. 28, and went back to J.H.S. 178. She was usually late getting back to school from lunch, but her teachers understood why and didn't scold her.

At the end of the school day, Shirley again picked up her sisters and took them home. It would be several hours until Mrs. St. Hill arrived, and those hours between school and evening are the ones that the mothers of latch-key children fear most. Shirley recalls, "She told us to go straight home at the end of the day, lock the door, and not open it for anyone until she got home. We sat in the front window, watching for the first glimpse of her.

When she came in sight we always screamed out in excitement, and the landlord downstairs would always shout, 'Shut up!'"

Perhaps the fact that she was once a latch-key child herself is one reason Shirley became such a strong proponent of day care. Perhaps the fact that her mother once worked as a domestic is one reason Shirley became a strong backer of unions for domestics; a union could help domestic servants gain better benefits and working conditions. There is no doubt that her experiences during the depression made Shirley more determined than ever to succeed and never again be poor.

Nearly all the money Mr. and Mrs. St. Hill earned went toward the rent. Food was scarce, and many nights the girls went to bed hungry. What they did eat was often not very nourishing. Every Thursday Mrs. St. Hill gave Shirley a quarter and sent her to the neighborhood bakery to buy items marked down as stale—bread, rolls, pie, cake enough for the next week. On other days Shirley or Mrs. St. Hill checked the greengrocers for wilted vegetables they could also buy inexpensively. Meat was a rare luxury, and the St. Hills ate only the cheapest cuts.

In the area of clothing they were lucky. An expert seamstress, Mrs. St. Hill could mend even the worst rip, and when she came across a bargain on material, she quickly turned it into a much-needed garment for one of her children. The white families for whom she worked in Flatbush sometimes gave her old clothing and leftover food—she nearly always arrived home carrying a brown paper bag that contained something her family could use.

But she and Mr. St. Hill always arrived home so tired. The girls, even Selma, the youngest, sensed their struggle. There was less laughter in the apartment, less conversation at the dinner table. But neither Charles nor Ruby St. Hill complained very often about their poverty, and if the children complained, their parents reminded them that there were many, many others who were worse off than they. At least they had a roof over their heads; at least they had some food and some clothing; at least their parents had jobs of some sort. There were many families in Bedford-Stuyvesant who faced eviction from their apartments and who had to depend upon charitable organizations and church relief centers for their food and clothing. Across the East River in Manhattan, the Black people of Harlem rioted in 1937, smashing and burning and looting community stores out of the sheer frustration and desperation and hopelessness of hunger and poverty.

The St. Hills were much better off in material ways. They were also much better off in another way. They never lost their hope. They never lost sight of their dream for the success of their children. There was always hope for the children and concern for their progress at school. Mr. St. Hill never neglected to ask each of his daughters what she had learned at school that day and never ceased to expect a detailed answer. For her part, Mrs. St. Hill did all she could to ensure her daughters' progress. Tired as she was from her job doing housework for other people, she never asked the girls to do more than a few light chores. They did much less work at home in Brooklyn than they had in Barbados. "You do your homework for school and read your library books," she would say. "I'll take care of the chores."

Reading was greatly stressed in the St. Hill household. The girls received few birthday and Christmas gifts, especially during the depression, but those gifts they did receive were books. Each one had her own dictionary, and as the years passed each had her own small library. Most of the books they received were the children's adventure type, such as Nancy Drew mysteries or Bobbsey Twins stories. The St. Hill girls were also faithful, if sometimes reluctant, patrons of the neighborhood library. Every other Saturday Mrs. St. Hill would take the girls to the library, where each was expected to check out the three books allowed. During the next two weeks, their mother would frequently ask how their reading was progressing, for they were expected to have read all three books before their next trip to the library.

Portrait of Harriet Tubman, ca. 1868–9. *Photograph by Benjamin F. Powelson. Courtesy of the Library of Congress.*

At first the books Shirley borrowed from the library were adventure stories, but as she entered junior high school she began to borrow books of a different sort— biographies of important men and women in American history. Through the tutoring she had received to enable her to catch up to her grade level, Shirley had become fascinated by American history. Next to English and spelling, it became her best subject. But she was not taught enough in school to satisfy her interest. She wanted to know more about the people her teachers mentioned, and so she began to borrow books on their lives from the library. At first, she read biographies of various Presidents and of men such as Benjamin Franklin. But gradually her interest, narrowed to the lives of important Black people in American history. In the 1930s, when Shirley was going to school, no Black history was taught. The only mention of Blacks occurred when slavery was discussed. Shirley and her sisters were luckier than some of their Black friends, for Charles St. Hill was very well read and knowledgeable about Black history. And the stress their parents had always placed upon reading had given them the ability to find out for themselves what they wanted to know. Shirley read many books on important Blacks, and from this reading she became especially interested in one of them. Not surprisingly, this person was a woman. A child identifies most strongly with people whom he or she can realistically aspire to be like. Harriet Tubman was both Black and female.

Born a slave, Harriet Tubman had escaped slavery and gone to the North. But she had not been content merely to gain her own freedom; she determined to help other slaves become free. She became one of the "conductors" on the Underground Railroad, a network of white abolitionists and free Blacks that operated prior to and during the Civil War. Routes were established between the slave states and the North along which were "way stations," or homes of people sympathetic to the cause. Harriet Tubman, dressed in men's clothing and usually traveling by night, would make her way south to slave plantations. There she would gather together a group of slaves who had the courage to attempt an escape and lead them secretly from one way station, where they found food and a place to sleep, to another until they had reached the free states.

Her code name was Moses, for like Moses in the Old Testament, she led the slaves out of the wilderness of slavery. She made numerous trips and was so successful that she became a living legend. White slaveholders put a price on her head, offering a reward for her capture dead or alive. She was never caught, and perhaps one reason was that the slaveholders were looking for a man. They could not believe Moses might be a woman. Shirley particularly liked that part because she was beginning to have a feminist consciousness. Although she had first become interested in Harriet Tubman as a Black, reading about this extraordinary woman had caused her to become interested in other great women in history.

This interest led her to Susan B. Anthony, a white woman who had been born in 1820, the very same year as Harriet Tubman. Susan Anthony became a leader of the first women's movement, campaigning to win for women the right to vote. Like others in the women's movement, she was also an abolitionist, a fighter against slavery. Many women equated their status in society with that of the Black slaves. They did not feel they could fight for their own rights without fighting for the slaves' rights as well. Once Susan Anthony's house in Rochester, New York, served as a way station for Harriet Tubman's Underground Railroad. For her part, Harriet Tubman supported the suffragist movement and often shared the speakers' platform with Susan Anthony at women's suffrage and abolitionist meetings.

Portrait of Susan B. Anthony, ca. 1870. *Photograph by Mathew B. Brady. Courtesy of the Library of Congress.*

Shirley read everything she could about both her heroines, and the more she read the more fascinated she was by the courage and the strength of these women. They were just as brave and strong as any of the men whose biographies she had read—

more so, because they also had to fight against the stigma of being women. It is an American tradition to go to jail for a cause, but the sight of Susan B. Anthony and other suffragists going to jail had shocked America—because they were women. A favorite way for those who opposed women's suffrage to break up meetings was to hire other women to create a particularly "female" disturbance. These women would, for example, jump up on chairs and begin to scream that there were mice in the room. The press would gleefully report the disturbance as just one more example of women's silliness and unfitness for the responsibility of voting. Harriet Tubman must have resented the fact that the slaveholders refused to believe a woman was helping so many of their slaves to escape—even though she was safer because of it.

Shirley could identify with their struggle. Although she was only in junior high school, she felt discriminated against because she was a girl. She made higher grades than all the boys in her class, and yet she knew they considered her "just a girl." At that age the boys tended to dislike girls anyway, although by high school they would feel quite differently. But Shirley sensed that their disdain for girls went deeper than mere adolescent standoffishness. This attitude was understandable. There were many more biographies of important men in history than of important women. There were many more stories about men in the newspapers than about women. A boy could say, "When I grow up, I want to be president of the United States," and although his friends would laugh at him, they would be aware that it was at least possible. If a girl said the same thing, her listeners would fall on the floor laughing, in a way that one can laugh only at an idea that is downright impossible. Shirley sensed this inequality of the sexes, and it bothered her at times, but in junior high school she did not think about it too often. Political consciousness was a long way off for adolescents, particularly young girls and Blacks. For now, Shirley was content to read about and idolize people such as Harriet Tubman and Susan B. Anthony.

Charles and Ruby St. Hill encouraged Shirley's independent reading because they understood that her reading about successful people further reinforced their own values. Charles St. Hill encouraged his daughter for a different reason as well—he had a pure desire for learning that Shirley seemed to have inherited.

Like her father, Shirley was a voracious reader, reading everything and anything she came across. By the time she was in junior high school, she was contributing to his dinner-time lectures, asking questions, making comments based upon her reading and what she had learned in school. "Visitors would always pick me out as the brightest one in the family," Shirley recalls.

In the other girls' eyes it must have been clear that their father too had picked Shirley out as the brightest one. He took her to Marcus Garvey tributes held by various Black organizations. At these meetings she heard the first Black nationalist talk she had ever heard, and it caused her to ask her father more questions and to make more associations with the things she had read. The special bond between Shirley and her father was unmistakable, and the other girls resented it.

Shirley graduated from J.H.S. 178 in June 1939. The following September she entered Girls' High School on Nostrand Avenue. The school had an excellent reputation, and only those girls who graduated at the top of their ninth-grade classes could attend. Girls from all over Brooklyn went there, some traveling long distances. At first the school was a rather long walk for Shirley, but shortly after she entered it the family moved again, this time to Patchen Avenue, very close to the school.

Exterior of the Girls' High School on Nostrand, 1900s. Detroit Publishing Co. *Courtesy of NYC AGO.*

Meeting the rent payments on the Ralph Avenue apartment had been a constant struggle for Charles and Ruby St. Hill, and Ruby had at last decided that it just was not worth the trouble. Her girls were growing; Shirley and Odessa, particularly, needed rooms of their own. After months of searching they finally found a larger apartment that they could afford, still in Bedford-Stuyvesant. It had six rooms, and through an agreement with the landlord, Charles St. Hill was able to obtain it rent-free in exchange for doing the janitorial work in the building. Now Ruby St. Hill could stay home again, and Shirley would no longer have to be a latch-key child. Another advantage, at least in Shirley's eyes, was the short walk to Girls' High.

Although the neighborhood was nearly all Black, Girls' High was about half white. By that age, of course, the students were aware of their racial differences, but those differences were not particularly stressed. Scholarship was heavily emphasized, and the absence of boys meant the absence of a major source of competition among high school age girls. Shirley did very well academically at Girls' High, winning a French medal. Her self-confidence and assertiveness made her a natural leader, and at a time when Black students were rarely elected to offices, she was vice-president of an honor society.

Although Shirley had always been self-confident, her pride in herself as a Black person increased during her high school years—again not as a result of what she learned at school but as a result of her own reading. "I had managed to find some books in the public library about our African heritage that few people then studied or talked about; I knew about the Ashanti kingdoms, for instance," Shirley recalls. Nowadays, Black history is taught in many schools, and Black studies departments have been established in colleges and universities across the country. Countless books written by and about Blacks on Black history and culture are available in libraries and bookstores.

The Black consciousness movement of the 1960s and 1970s has made most Blacks aware of their rich African heritage, of the age before slavery when Africa was a land of highly civilized and literate kingdoms such as those of the Ashanti tribe. But in the early 1940s a young Black girl like Shirley had to search intensively to find her heritage, to learn about the history of her people. Understandably, many young Blacks did not bother. Shirley did, and her pride in the heritage of her people grew with every book she read.

Shirley also found living Black people of whom she could be proud. At that time every Black American had at least one Black hero—Joe Louis, the Brown Bomber, the heavyweight champion of the world. But although Shirley was just as pleased as any other Black person when Joe Louis won a fight, she looked for heroes and heroines of another sort. She found W. E. B. Du Bois, probably the greatest Black scholar of the twentieth century. He had been the first Black to earn a Ph.D. at Harvard University, and by 1940 he had published a half dozen noted works on Black history and Black life in America. A champion of civil rights, he did not appeal to the emotions, as Marcus Garvey had, but to the mind. Shirley read most of his books and yearned to meet him. She considered him the most brilliant writer she had ever read.

Adam Clayton Powell, Jr., unknown date. *Photograph by James J. Kriegman. Courtesy of Wikimedia Commons and the Library of Congress.*

Closer to home Shirley found Adam Clayton Powell, Jr. Assistant to his father, Adam Clayton Powell, Sr., pastor of Harlem's Abyssinian Baptist Church, Adam, Jr. had been deeply affected by the Harlem riot of 1937. He had questioned the reasons behind the riot and had come up with an answer: the Black people of Harlem had looted and burned their own community because it wasn't really their community. They lived in it, but whites owned the stores, worked in the stores, and took home the money Blacks spent in those stores. With other community leaders, Adam Powell began a massive campaign to get the white store owners of Harlem to hire Black workers. When this campaign was successful, he organized a similar movement to force the bus and telephone companies to hire Blacks. Charles St. Hill and Shirley had read with great interest the newspaper accounts of the campaigns being waged across the river and wished that Bedford-Stuyvesant had a leader like Adam Clayton Powell. When in 1941 Powell became the first Black to be elected to the New York City Council, they were almost as pleased as if a Black from Bedford-Stuyvesant had been elected to the council.

But Shirley's major present-day idol was a Black woman. Her name was Mary McLeod Bethune. When Shirley was in high school, Mary Bethune was a trusted friend and adviser of President Franklin Delano Roosevelt. As a young woman, she had founded a school for Black girls in Florida, a school that later became the coeducational Bethune-Cookman College. She was founder and president of the National Council of Negro Women, a vice-president of the National Association for the Advancement of Colored People (NAACP), a director of the Division of Negro Affairs for the National Youth Administration, and a special adviser to the president on minority affairs. Shirley searched the newspapers and magazines for pictures of this tall, dignified, Black woman and for articles that mentioned her name. While she could admire W. E. B. Du Bois and applaud Adam Clayton Powell, she could dream about being an important woman like Mary Bethune. She hoped she would have an important-sounding name like Mary McLeod Bethune. Shirley St. Hill—.

Portrait of Mary McLeod Bethune, 1949. *Photograph by Carl Van Vechten. Courtesy of the Library of Congress.*

For all her scholarship and independent reading, Shirley was not a bookish sort who cared nothing for social life. In fact she would have liked to have had a very active social life if her mother had allowed it. But Ruby St. Hill had very definite ideas about what was and wasn't proper for a young girl.

Shirley loved music. Next to her father and her books it was probably the most important thing in her life. Ruby St. Hill had encouraged this love, managing to find a secondhand piano and the money to pay for lessons for Shirley. Shirley also loved to dance, but this her mother did not encourage, because dancing would mean being with boys, and Ruby St. Hill strongly discouraged her daughters' seeing boys.

She was terribly strict about their going out—or even being late from school—so strict that sometimes her husband reminded her, "Ruby you must remember these are American kids, not island kids. You are here in America." But his wishes had no effect. "Charles," she would answer, "we've got to be strict with them if we want them to grow up to be something." Ruby allowed the girls to go to school programs and to a few parties, but they had to be home by ten o'clock. Shirley was allowed to have boys to the apartment, but after the first few times she decided it was not worth the embarrassment. "They had to leave by ten o'clock," she recalls, "and if they didn't, Mother took direct action. She came in the parlor in her nightgown and started pulling down the shades."

Shirley complained to her father about her lack of freedom, but in this area he could not help her. "When your mother has her mind set. . ." he would sigh. Shirley watched her friends doing things she was forbidden to do; she listened to the girls at school talk about their dates. Shirley had never had a date—her mother would not allow it. She rebelled in little ways. She started trying to play jazz tunes on the piano. She learned all the latest dance steps, like the lindyhop, and practiced them to perfection. At school dances, which her mother allowed her to attend as long as she was home by ten o'clock, she often won prizes. What struck the judges even more than her skill was the way she threw herself into the dance. They did not know she was dancing out her frustration. But she never defied her mother. She graduated from high school without ever having had a real date.

3.
BROOKLYN COLLEGE

Shirley graduated from Girls' High in June 1942. The speakers at the graduation ceremonies exhorted the outgoing class to do something important in the world, for they had a precious gift—an excellent education. Shirley listened, but in her own mind she knew that a good education was not necessarily a key that would open all doors. Money would help. Although she had received scholarship offers from Vassar College and Oberlin College, two of the best colleges in the country, she had been unable to accept them. Her parents, though bursting with pride that their daughter's excellent grades had earned her such coveted scholarships, had sadly reminded her that they just did not have the money to pay the expenses not covered by the scholarships. Shirley was disappointed, but she knew they were right. Both colleges were out of town so that she would have had to live in a dormitory and pay for her meals. Neither scholarship covered living or travel expenses. Reluctantly, she had chosen to go to Brooklyn College, one of the five city-run colleges. Tuition was free, and she could travel there and back each day by subway. The only expense would be her books.

As Shirley listened to the graduation speakers, she also thought to herself that success would be easier for her if she were white. She looked around at her white classmates. Some planned to be lawyers, nurses, social workers. She knew those occupations were pretty much closed to her. Law schools and medical schools did admit Blacks on occasion, but it was hard enough for Black men to enroll; a Black woman would have little chance. Social work had not been opened to Blacks as yet, and when Blacks began to be admitted, it would be Black men who were allowed in first. Shirley might at times have thought briefly of trying to enter these fields, but she was a realistic eighteen-year-old. As she recalls, "My youth may have been sheltered from boys and some other realities, but I was Black, and nobody needed to draw me a diagram." Teaching was the only profession that a young Black woman could hope to pursue, and Shirley had already made up her mind to become a teacher.

This is not to say that she was pessimistic about her future. Indeed, she was very hopeful. She still possessed the self-confidence that seems to have been hers since the age of three. She was bright, she was proud, and she was determined to be successful. She was determined to be somebody.

In the fall of 1942 Shirley entered Brooklyn College. She will never forget those first bewildering days. The college was one of the largest city-run institutions, and Shirley was taken aback by the thousands of students hurrying to and fro, all seeming to know where they were going. She also noticed warily that the great majority of the students were white. Later she found out that there were only about sixty Black students attending the day session. She knew that a student was required either to have a high average or else do well on an entrance exam to enroll in the college, but because it was a tuition-free "subway college," she had expected to find more fellow Black students. It took her a while to realize that most Black children in New York City had not been given the excellent schooling she had. They had not received their early schooling in Barbados, and they had fallen behind their white classmates in elementary school. Once behind in elementary school, they had stayed behind through high school, and if they had graduated at all it was with averages far below those required by the city college system. Then, too, most Black children did not have parents like Charles and Ruby St. Hill, parents whose highest goal was their children's education and who expected their children to share that goal.

Also bewildering to her was the great amount of political activity at Brooklyn College. Bulletin-board notices announced political meetings, and speakers stood on the steps of buildings or on hastily assembled platforms and harangued passing students. Leaflets advocating this or that cause were constantly thrust at her. Shirley had never seen so much political activity, and she wondered if she would ever understand what it was all about.

Photograph of Brooklyn College downtown campus at 66 Court Street. Date unknown. *Courtesy of Brooklyn College.*

In the beginning she did not even try. As the first in either the Seale or St. Hill families to go to college, she was aware that she had a great responsibility to her parents as well as to herself to do well. She wisely avoided joining clubs at school until she had adjusted to the college routine and to what was expected of her by her teachers. She would have enjoyed a bit of social life, but her mother saw to it that she did not. The high school rules about boys and dates and parties were not relaxed. Shirley spent most of her time in the college library and made no new friends.

Shirley's grades were excellent her first year at Brooklyn College, and in her second year she felt she could join some of the myriad activities at the school. The year before, some Black upperclassmen had started the first all-Black student group, the Harriet Tubman Society, and this was the first group she joined. Naturally she was attracted to a group of fellow Blacks, and she was particularly interested in a group that had named itself after one of her early heroines.

The group was very political and very race conscious. Shirley had not heard such strong talk about white oppression, Black racial consciousness, and Black pride from anyone except her father, and she listened with intense interest. For a long time she did not contribute to the talk about Black-white relations, but she did find she could contribute to the discussions on Black pride. There was a great deal she had learned from her reading about Harriet Tubman, W. E. B. Du Bois, and other important Blacks in history as well as about the ancient African kingdoms that the others did not know, and they came to respect her for her knowledge. But Shirley learned from the others as well. Partly because of their influence and partly because the overwhelming majority of students were white, Shirley began to look at things and situations more and more from a Black point of view.

Although Shirley planned to be a teacher, she took no education courses during her four years at Brooklyn College. Instead she majored in sociology, even though she knew she could not become a sociologist, and she minored in Spanish. In her sociology classes the teachers spoke of Blacks as an inferior group of people, and the sociology texts spoke of them as a "problem" for sociologists. Shirley would look around at her fellow students, almost all white, and see them nodding their heads in agreement. Sitting there and listening, she would feel strange and angry.

She had similar experiences in the Political Science Society, which she also joined in her sophomore year. Although the society considered itself very liberal and progressive, its speakers regularly spoke of Blacks as somehow less human than whites and requiring their benevolence.

"For a long time I watched such white people closely," Shirley recalled, "listened to them, and observed silently the treatment Blacks were given in social and political situations. It grew on me that we, Black men especially, were expected to be subservient even in groups where ostensibly everyone was equal. Blacks played by those rules; if a white man walked in, they [Blacks] came subtly to attention. But I could see their fear, helplessness, and discomfort."

With each new experience of white prejudice and Black humility Shirley became more and more angry, and more and more frustrated. She wanted to do something to show whites that Black people were as good as they were, but what could she do? She realized that racism was woven into the very fabric of American life—how could one young Black woman hope to change things? Yet the knowledge that a task was practically impossible had never stopped Shirley or the rest of her family from trying. When she was three and her mother had placed the sewing machine far out of reach, Shirley had piled up boxes and chairs until she could reach it. When Charles and Ruby's dream for an education for their children had seemed unattainable, they became even more determined to make the dream come true. Shirley realized she was not in a position to make a major impression upon whites, but she was determined to do whatever she could.

She and other Black female students formed a club that Shirley named Ipothia, "in pursuit of the highest of all." White sororities would not allow Blacks in their membership, and Ipothia would show these white sororities that the Black female students did not need them. At the same time, at Shirley's urging, the Harriet Tubman Society began a campaign to expose the all-white student clubs.

She joined the Debating Society, unconcerned that her slight lisp was always noticeable to her listeners. "They don't have any trouble understanding what I have to say," she said to those who suggested she take speech classes to correct the problem. In a short time the Debating Society had become her favorite extracurricular activity. Shirley had always loved to talk and to persuade others to see her point of view. Her favorite debating subjects were discrimination and prejudice. Although she realized she did not always convince her white listeners that Blacks were equal to whites and entitled to all the rights and privileges they enjoyed, she felt sure she made an impression on some of them.

Because of her increasing skill at debating and her excellent work in her political science classes, one of her political science professors, Louis Warsoff, became interested in Shirley. They began to have long talks about the world, about America, and about people. Professor Warsoff, who was blind, was the only man other than her father with whom Shirley had ever experienced a close relationship. The relationship came at a fortunate time, for Professor Warsoff was white. In her anger and frustration over discrimination and prejudice, Shirley had developed many antiwhite feelings. As she would later recall,

"He was one of the first white men whom I ever really knew and trusted…From Professor Warsoff I learned that white people were not really different from me."

1959 Broeklundian, page 111. Louis Warsoff is in the bottom right corner. *Courtesy of Brooklyn College.*

Her distrust of whites abated somewhat because of her friendship with Professor Warsoff. Shirley began to use her energy and her debating skill in another cause—the campaigns of white female students for student government office. She painted posters, organized rallies, wrote speeches, and made speeches herself. Her candidates did not win—women were just not elected to campus offices at Brooklyn College in the early 1940s—but not because of any lack of effort on Shirley's part.

Knowing where Shirley Chisholm is now, it is easy to see how her years at Brooklyn College were preparing her to become involved in politics. Majoring in sociology was showing her how different groups of people behave among themselves and relate to society; belonging to the Debating Society was helping her to develop her public speaking ability; organizing Ipothia and taking an active role in the Harriet Tubman Society were helping her to increase her leadership ability; working to elect women to campus offices was giving her experience in campaigning. Yet at the time Shirley had no thought of becoming really involved in politics.

Once, after she had starred in a debate, Professor Warsoff had said, "You ought to go into politics."

"I was astonished by his naïveté," Shirley remembers.

"'Proffy,' I said, 'you forget two things. I'm Black—and I'm a woman.'"

But Professor Warsoff's remark stayed with Shirley. She realized that he had somehow underlined and brought to her attention a thought she had kept so far back in her mind that she had not really known it was there. She was indeed interested in politics. Even if she did not feel she could ever run for office herself, she did want to become involved in some way.

She began to go to political club meetings. In those years New York politics was the political clubs, which were organized by state assembly districts. Although both political parties had clubs, the Democrats had many more, and in most parts of the city "club" meant the Democratic club. The club served many purposes. It was a place for those in power in the district to meet and plan strategies. It was a place for people in the district to take their problems and get advice or help—in exchange for their promise to vote the way the club leaders told them. But it was by no means an organization devoted to serving the people. Many clubs did not allow Blacks in unless they were brought by a white member. Even all-white or nearly all-white clubs were strongly divided between leaders and ordinary citizens who came seeking help; the ordinary citizens were made somehow to feel like beggars. The Seventeenth Assembly District Club in Brooklyn was two-thirds Black, yet the leadership was white. Blacks sat on one side of the room, whites on the other. Whites who joined the club did so expecting to somehow someday hold powerful offices in the citywide and statewide Democratic organizations. Blacks who joined the club could expect little more than the most minor positions.

Shirley understood all this after going to only one or two meetings at the 17th A.D. Club to hear certain speakers in whom she was interested. She saw that Blacks were expected to stay "in their place." They were not even supposed to ask questions when a speaker called for them. Shirley thought that ridiculous. *She* would not stay in her place—she did ask questions.

> "I asked the sanitation commissioner why trash wasn't picked up regularly in Bedford-Stuyvesant, as it was in white neighborhoods. I asked councilmen why they hadn't delivered on their pro mises. Such questions were unwelcome, and after the meeting someone was likely to tell me so. I pretended innocence: How do I know what kind of questions you're supposed to ask? But I knew very well, and so did they, that I was needling them to show how little they did or cared for the people who kept them in office."

Shirley felt very strongly that predominantly Black districts should be represented by Blacks, not by whites, but the white Democratic organization seemed so powerful that no one could overcome it. Then, in her senior year, she met a man who felt as she did and was determined to wrest some of the power away from the whites in the organization. His name was Wesley McD. Holder. Shirley had heard of this man before. He was a native of

British Guiana who had been active in Brooklyn politics since the 1930s. After working in Washington, he had returned to Brooklyn to organize a drive to get Blacks chosen as candidates for elective office. Listening to him talk of his plans, Shirley began to feel hopeful that perhaps this man could succeed. But at the time, Holder's idea was little more than an idea. It was not enough of a reality to make Shirley increase her involvement in politics.

Shirley took on a number of other community projects. She volunteered to work with children at an Urban League settlement house, teaching art and sewing classes, and writing and producing skits and plays. She went to hospitals to read to old people and to organize entertainment for them. She joined the Brooklyn chapter of the NAACP, which was working to combat discrimination in hiring, working conditions, pay, and promotion. She became so busy that she was hardly ever at home. If she was not volunteering to work for some community organization or institution, she was at a meeting of the Harriet Tubman Society or Ipothia or the Debating Society; if she was not there, she was at class or at the college library, where she spent long hours studying to maintain her excellent grades.

Shirley's mother complained that she was practically a stranger in the house, and it is likely that this situation was fine with Shirley. For years she had not gotten along very well with her mother and sisters. She resented her mother's continued strictness about her social life, and her sisters resented her special relationship with her father. In fact, Shirley seems to have deliberately become active in outside activities so that she would not have to spend very much time at home, where the St. Hill family had again outgrown its space.

Ironically, if Shirley's extreme busyness was partly due to her resentment of her mother's strictness, it also prevented her from having what little social life would have been allowed her. She did go to dances, and was well known as an excellent dancer. Young men were eager to have her as their partner, especially in dance contests. But away from dances she was usually shunned by boys. True, she was not particularly pretty, but she was energetic and full of a vitality that made her sparkle. Men considered her unapproachable because she was too busy, too active—she seemed not to need them. "Young men had always dropped me," she would recall. "If we were dancing, I'd talk about some world problem or other. I had a reputation of being too intellectual."

The only males who seemed to consider Shirley's intellectualism attractive were Professor Warsoff and her father. Shirley tried to be at home whenever her father was there. They would have long talks—Shirley now contributing as much as her father because of her experiences and activities at college. World War II had begun in 1939 and the United States had entered it in 1941. Shirley and her father discussed discrimination against Blacks in the armed forces and the irony of the slogan that victory would make "the world safe for democracy" when American Blacks did not yet share in the fruits of democracy.

Across the East River in Manhattan, Adam Clayton Powell, Jr. had waged a successful campaign in 1941 to become the first Black member of the New York City Council, where he pressed for laws against discrimination in many areas. Then in 1944 he announced his candidacy for the United States congressional seat from the new Eighteenth Congressional District in Harlem. Shirley and her father followed the campaign closely, and when Powell won in November 1944, they and many other Black New Yorkers felt as if it were a personal victory.

Charles St. Hill was at home practically as little as his daughter at this time. He was working overtime at the burlap bag factory as often as he could, for his savings account was mounting, and his and Ruby's second goal in life—their own home—was in sight. When in 1945 he had at last painfully saved $10,000 from his wages, he bought a house—a solid, three-story one on Prospect Place in Brooklyn. The St. Hill family moved for the last time—into their very own home. On the first evening they were settled in, there was a small family celebration. Charles and Ruby St. Hill, tired and worn from their years of struggle but happy and triumphant, stood with their arms around each other. Charles said to his daughters, "Your mother and I have worked hard and we have accomplished our two goals in life. If you work hard and never lose sight of your goals, you can do the same." Shirley listened and understood, but she knew her goals would be more ambitious than those of her parents. What those goals would be, she was still not sure.

She had decided to devote her life to children. Her work at the Urban League settlement house had convinced her that her decision to become a teacher had been a good one. She had decided not to devote much time to Black community organizations such as the NAACP. She would later recall, "Even as an undergraduate, I was beginning to feel how useless it was for Blacks to sit and talk with 'the leading people' in the community on biracial committees. It had begun to be clear that as long as we kept talking, nothing much was going to happen, and that this was what the 'leading people' really wanted." Beyond these decisions Shirley was unsure of her goals. How could she define her vague desire to be somebody as a goal?

All during her senior year Shirley continued her myriad activities, keeping so busy that she hardly had time to think about herself or the future. If she had stopped to think, she would have realized that deep down she was rather lonely and unhappy. She had still never had a real date, and as more and more of her classmates became pinned, or engaged, she sometimes wondered if she ever would. Her embarrassment over her mother's strictness had caused her to erect barriers around herself. She would reject young men before they had the opportunity to reject her. Boys her own age shied away from her. It took an older man to understand her.

She met him during spring vacation in her senior year. She had a temporary job at a jewelry factory in Manhattan, and every day she boarded the subway with a bag lunch and strict orders from her mother not to socialize with the other employees. But one handsome, older man, a Jamaican, refused to be snubbed. Shirley began to have lunch with him, and when spring vacation was over and Shirley left the factory, he came to visit her in Brooklyn.

Ruby St. Hill did not approve of the man. She said he dressed too casually for a formal call to a girl's home. There were other reasons she did not trust him, but they were vague and undefined. When Shirley heard no other concrete reasons for her mother's dislike for the Jamaican, she refused to take it seriously. She felt her mother wanted her to be a spinster. The two battled until Shirley gave an ultimatum: if her mother forbade her to see the older man, she would pack up and move out. From then on, the two maintained, in Shirley's words, "an armed truce" on the matter. She and the man began to date steadily.

Shirley graduated cum laude from Brooklyn College in June 1946. Immediately she began looking for a job as a teacher. She visited elementary school after elementary school, but each time she was turned down, even for a job as a teacher's aide. The problem, she learned, was that although she was nearly twenty-two, she was so tiny that she looked only about sixteen or seventeen. The administrators at the schools did not feel that she looked old enough to be able to discipline the students. When her protests were of no avail, Shirley thought, Well, if I look too young to teach grammar school, perhaps I look old enough to teach nursery school. She began to make the rounds of the nursery schools and daycare centers, but she met the same reaction there. Finally she blew up. "Don't judge me by my size! Put me on probation and judge me by what I can do!" At last she was able to persuade the director of the Mt. Calvary Child Care Center in Harlem to hire her on a probationary basis. As she had known, once she was able to show what she could do with children, she was hired on a permanent basis.

4.

MARRIAGE, CAREER, AND LOCAL POLITICS

Shirley did not have to work long at the daycare center to know she had chosen the right career. She was helping children to learn, to get a head start in school, and she was helping their mothers as well. Mothers with children at the daycare center did not have to hang keys around their children's necks and leave them to fend for themselves as Mrs. St. Hill had done with Shirley. They could go to work knowing their children were safe and well cared for.

Once sure that she would follow a teaching career, Shirley took steps to become as well qualified as possible. She enrolled in the master's degree program at Columbia University. Nearly every day after the daycare center closed, Shirley grabbed a bite to eat and took the subway to Columbia University for night classes. After class she took the long subway ride home to Brooklyn, falling into bed exhausted after her long and busy day. Weekends were devoted to studying, for she had little time during the week to do so.

Despite her heavy work and school schedule, Shirley continued many of her community activities, such as reading to the aged. She also continued to go to 17th A. D. Club meetings and soon joined the club. As a member she was expected to work on club projects, and as a woman she was expected to work on the projects for which the women members were responsible. Her first assignment was to find and decorate cigar boxes to be used to hold raffle tickets and money collected at the club's annual card party and raffle. This was not at all Shirley's idea of political involvement. When she mentioned this to a veteran club woman, the woman replied, "Dear, someone must do these

Aerial photograph of Columbia University campus, 1952. *Photograph by Angelo Rizzuto. Courtesy of the Library of Congress.*

things. Everyone should do what she can to help. Why, our annual raffle and card party is the club's biggest fund raiser." But this answer did not satisfy Shirley. As far as she was concerned, her talents and those of the other women were being wasted. Her speeches today, particularly those to women's groups, stress this theme:

"You see women going about communities collecting monies for different kinds of drives, coming together to have parties, dinners, and luncheons in order to raise funds for a particular cause in which they are interested. Well, that same kind of talent and energy needs to be utilized on broader levels today in America."

"Although women in this country, for the most part, have been the envelope stuffers, have been the ones who have given the card parties to raise the monies in order that the gentlemen can go to different political offices, have gathered the petitions, have been the speech writers for many of the gentlemen, very few women in this country have actually been the standard-bearers for political parties."

Of course in the mid-1940s there were no women standard-bearers, and Shirley knew that this dream was a long way off. She was not foolish enough to try to goad the women members of the 17th A.D. Club into pushing for that kind of power. But there were things she thought they should push for.

The annual card party and raffle was indeed the major fund-raising event for the club, whose only other source of income was dues. Yet the men never offered any money to run the event. The women had to beg money here and there to provide prizes and print raffle books; they even had to beg cigar boxes! "This is ridiculous," Shirley told the other women on the committee. "They should provide us with a budget to work with." "You're absolutely right," they answered. "Why should we go out and beg when we raise so much money for the club?" The women demanded—and the men were forced to give them—a budget for the party.

From then on the women began to speak up a little more often and to listen to Shirley's opinions. From then on the men considered Shirley a troublemaker.

Meanwhile, a year or two after graduation, Shirley became engaged to the Jamaican man whom she had met at the jewelry factory and whom she had been dating steadily ever since. She did not think anyone could be as happy as she. She loved her job, was close to getting her master's degree from Columbia, and would soon marry the man she loved. They would have children and educate them, they would have a house, and she would have a professional career. She knew exactly where she was going.

Then the nightmare began. Her fiancé, she learned, was already married to a woman in Jamaica. He was deeply involved in immigration fraud as part of a phony-birth-certificate and blackmail ring. He was arrested by the U.S. Immigration and Naturalization Service and deported. Shirley's world toppled down around her.

Now Ruby St. Hill knew why she had distrusted this man from the start, but she did not say "I told you so" to her daughter. Shirley was taking the whole matter very badly. "The shock lasted for months," Shirley recalls. "I couldn't sleep; I couldn't eat. Far from plump to start with, I gradually became a skeleton. I considered suicide. I hated men and thought I always would. Life had nothing more to offer me that would ever be any good."

At least the family doctor urged a change of scene, and Shirley was taken to a farm in New Jersey owned by friends of the St. Hills'. There she did recuperate physically, and she returned to work at the daycare center and to finish her master's degree at Columbia. Still bitter over her unhappy love affair, she tended to avoid men. "I was always running from meeting to meeting. I never had time for young men." But the man she would eventually marry was willing to wait until she had time.

About a year before, Conrad Chisholm had stopped Shirley as she dashed from class at Columbia to a meeting. The two had talked, and while Shirley's intellectualism usually turned men off, "Conrad was fascinated," Shirley recalls. But though Shirley had considered the stocky, quiet Jamaican nice, she was already in love and was not interested. After her engagement ended in disaster, Conrad Chisholm tried to take up where he had left off, but Shirley wanted no part of it. She had been deeply hurt. The first man ever to be romantically interested in her had turned out to be married and a criminal. She would never trust another man; she would never again allow herself to be hurt.

But Conrad Chisholm persisted. For months he waited for her after class or after work or visited her at home, where Ruby welcomed him and Shirley ignored him. Calmly, patiently, gradually, he melted the wall of ice that Shirley had built around herself until she realized that he was a different kind of man, that he loved her and would not hurt her. They were married in 1949; Shirley was twenty-five.

They rented a small house in Brooklyn not far from Shirley's parents. Conrad continued in his job as a detective for a private security bureau specializing in insurance claims cases. Shirley continued as a full-fledged teacher at the Mt. Calvary Child Care Center. She also continued her political and community activities, which, even though they kept her away from home many evenings, did not seem to bother Conrad at all. Many husbands would resent the activities that kept their wives away from home; some would even be jealous. But Conrad Chisholm loved his wife and wanted her to do the things she enjoyed doing. He was not at all threatened by her outside interests or jealous as she rose in importance in 17th A.D. politics.

At the 17th A.D. Club she had kept on asking embarrassing questions, questions that others dared not ask. To her surprise, rather than trying to oust her from the club the leaders saw to it that she was elected to the board of directors and then to the position of third vice-president. But instead of sitting back smugly, resting on her laurels and ceasing to "rock the boat," as the leaders had expected, Shirley continued her troublemaking ways. In a short time she received a letter informing her that she was no longer on the board of directors.

The experience was an important political lesson for Shirley. It made her understand better the workings of the powerful. The one thing those in power did not need was a troublemaker. If they could not dispose of a troublemaker in some way, they took him or her in, expecting that being part of the inner circle, getting a piece of the power, was all the troublemaker wanted anyway and that he or she would then cease to agitate. That is what had happened with the Blacks who managed to get the few appointed positions open to them in the city government; that was why they never tried to use their position to bring about change or to help their fellow Blacks.

This tactic had not worked with Shirley. And being dismissed from the board of directors did not embarrass her into staying away. She went to the next club meeting as usual, to the astonishment of many of her fellow members. Charles St. Hill laughed and laughed when Shirley told him how she had confused the leaders of the 17th A.D. Club by refusing to play their game. He always enjoyed her political stories, and whenever she had time at night, Shirley would drop by the house on Prospect Place to tell her father of the latest "deals" being made at the club. Whenever she told an anecdote, she used her ability to mimic others to good advantage, assuming the characters of the people in the story. When she told what a fat, pompous club leader said, she stuck out her stomach and pushed her chin down on her chest to make a double chin. When she told about one of the important women in the club, she made her voice shrill and talked very fast. Another important woman wore many rings and spoke in a high-society accent; when speaking of this woman Shirley would make exaggerated gestures with her hands and pronounce her words with a bored drawl. Listening to Shirley's stories, Charles St. Hill felt as if he were participating in the intrigues of the 17th A.D. Club.

At first Shirley had urged him to go with her to meetings, but although he accepted from time to time, her father protested that he was a little too old to begin political activity. Besides, Ruby would complain her head off.

Ruby St. Hill had no interest in politics. In fact she disapproved of Shirley's involvement. After all, Shirley was a married woman now. Her daycare work was all right—they had sent her to college so that she might have a career. But at night she should stay at home with her husband. Ruby rarely listened to Shirley's political stories, and neither did the other girls. They had better things to do than listen to political talk. They really could not understand how their father and sister enjoyed it so much.

Although she maintained her membership in the 17th A.D. Club, Shirley gradually became less active in the club. She had a new interest. Wesley McD. Holder, with whom she had kept in touch since Brooklyn College, was trying to organize a group to work for a Black lawyer who had decided to run for the post of civil judge in the 1953 election. The regular Democratic Party in Brooklyn had brought in a white lawyer from outside Bedford-Stuyvesant as their candidate. For people like Holder and Shirley this was the last straw. As Bedford-Stuyvesant's population had become predominantly Black, the regular Democratic Party had continued to run only white candidates, but at least they had been from the area. Now, Bedford-Stuyvesant was nearly all Black and no likely white candidates were left, so the Party was going outside the neighborhood for candidates rather than support a Black man! When a local Black lawyer named Lewis Flagg decided to run for the judgeship, Holder saw a chance to challenge the power of the regular Democratic Party. He organized a group called the Committee for the Election of Lewis S. Flagg, Jr., and before long he had all the members he needed—Blacks who were fed up with the regular Democratic Party and some whites who were fed up too. But Flagg would need more than just a strong organization working for him— he would need votes as well. That, Holder explained to the committee, was their biggest task. They had to get the many Blacks in Bedford-Stuyvesant who were not registered voters to register and to vote. And they had to get those who were already registered voters to cast their ballots for Flagg. It was a big job. The Black residents of Bedford-Stuyvesant had been denied real participation in the election process for so long, it was hard to make them believe that now they really had a chance to participate and to make a difference. Some were so used to voting the straight Democratic line every election day that it was hard to convince them that an independent Black candidate had a chance to win.

Shirley spent long hours ringing doorbells, trying to convince people to register to vote, or, if they were already registered, to vote for Flagg. She used every argument she could think of: "There are forty-nine civil judges in Brooklyn; we think it's about time one of them was Black." "What do you mean the white man's got politics all sewn up? Over in Harlem, they elected Adam Clayton Powell to Congress! Now if the people in Harlem can do that, we ought to be able to elect a Black judge." "You don't owe the Brooklyn Democratic Party a thing; what have they done for us except keep us out of elections?" The more she tried to convince others that Flagg could win, the more Shirley convinced herself. Unity was all it took, and a sense of hope. Behind all those doors of Black homes and apartments was power—the power of the vote.

As the campaign wore on, Wesley McD. Holder was continually struck by the hard work and will to win of this young woman. She could be a real asset to any campaign, he decided, and he gave her more and more responsibility in the organization. Shirley used that responsibility to good advantage. As she would later say in a speech, "For much of my twenty years in politics … I was one of the 'party workers,' stuffing envelopes, organizing rallies, writing speeches and answering phones. But, above all, I watched and listened to the behind-the-scenes 'wheeling and dealing' that characterizes American politics and, perhaps, all politics." Although she didn't know it then, this behind-the-scenes knowledge would serve her well when she decided to enter politics herself.

Flagg won the election. Perhaps, Shirley thought, there was hope for Blacks in politics after all.

Though Shirley had been devoting as much time as possible to the Flagg campaign, she had also been busy pursuing her career as a teacher. In 1953 she had been appointed director of a private nursery school, the Friend in Need Nursery near Atlantic Avenue in Brooklyn. She had enjoyed being in charge and trying out some of her own ideas about teaching and caring for young children. In 1954 she was asked to become director of the large HamiltonMadison House Child Care Center in lower Manhattan. The

Friend in Need Day Nursery, 1916. *Courtesy of Brooklyn Daily Eagle photographs, Brooklyn Public Library, and the Center for Brooklyn History.*

center had a staff of twenty-four and 130 children between the ages of three and seven. As director, Shirley would have more responsibilities than she had ever had before, and she eagerly accepted the offer.

Shirley's own experiences going to school on Barbados, as well as her experience as a teacher's aide and a teacher at Mt. Calvary Child Care Center and as director of the private nursery school in Brooklyn, had given her very definite ideas about day care. Young children, she felt, should be treated with strictness tempered by warmth and love—the way Granny Seale had brought her up. Their day should be well structured: naps, play periods, lunch periods, and snack periods should occur at exactly the same time every day. They should be encouraged to learn to read and write just as early as possible—if she could do so by age four and a half, then so could other children. Many of the children of the Hamilton-Madison Center were Puerto Rican and knew little English. Shirley, believing that they should be taught English immediately, took personal charge of teaching many of the children. In return they taught her their language. Although Shirley had minored in Spanish at Brooklyn College, she found that Puerto Rican Spanish was different from the classical Spanish she had learned. Her "Spanish lessons" at the center would prove a great help to her in later years.

Although the staff at the Hamilton-Madison Center did not agree at first with many of Shirley's ideas, she managed to bring most of them around through numerous staff discussion meetings and a calm determination not to give in. The work was exhausting, but Shirley had never been happier. She knew she was doing something she was really cut out to do.

Meanwhile, Conrad Chisholm had been experiencing some career changes as well. In 1953 he had been offered a job doing investigative work for a large railroad company. It would mean a lot of traveling and being away from home for long periods of time, and he had discussed the offer with his wife. Shirley knew that she would sometimes be lonely with Conrad away, but she knew he wanted to accept the job and she would never try to hold him back. In their four years of marriage Shirley and Conrad Chisholm had achieved something very special. They had built a life together and at the same time had been able to pursue their separate careers. Just as Conrad did not complain about Shirley's political work, Shirley did not complain when Conrad took a job that frequently kept him away from home.

With Conrad gone so much, Shirley had devoted a great deal of time to the Committee for the Election of Lewis S. Flagg, Jr. When Flagg won, she was eager to help keep up the momentum the organization had created. Wesley McD. Holder felt the same way, of course. In many ways Flagg's victory had been Holder's victory, for he had organized the movement to support Flagg. In 1954 Holder organized the Bedford-Stuyvesant

Lewis S. Flagg, Jr., ca. 1949-54. *Courtesy of Brooklyn Daily Eagle photographs, Brooklyn Public Library, and the Center for Brooklyn History.*

Political League (BSPL) in the hope of continuing the successful activity that had resulted in Flagg's election. The BSPL ran a full slate of candidates in the 1954 elections under the slogan, "Let's Make History Again!" But none of the candidates won. They ran full slates the next year and the next and the next. Holder himself ran for various offices, but nothing seemed to bring back the magic of the Flagg campaign. Shirley remained in the regular Democratic 17th A.D. Club, but she devoted most of her time to the BSPL. She was a moving force, leading delegations to city hall and speaking at rallies. She became vice-president of the league, and by 1958 many people were urging her to run against Holder for the presidency.

At first she declined. Mac, as she called Holder, had always been president. He had founded the BSPL, and he had been active for many years before that in pushing for Black political influence in Brooklyn. Anyone who ran against him did not have much chance of winning and had a good chance of gaining Holder as a lifetime enemy. But after a while Shirley reconsidered. Although she did not feel she could win the presidency of the BSPL, she did feel she had a right to run. That was what democracy was all about.

When Holder heard of Shirley's decision, he was furious. He felt that she was being disloyal to him, that she had "turned on him." The campaign was a bitter one. Holder stressed all the things he had done for Shirley and asked the members of the BSPL if this was any way to repay him. Shirley listed her activities on behalf of the organization and reminded the members that its constitution contained no provision that Holder be president for life. But she knew that in a way he was right. He had taught her most of what she knew about politics. In the end he proved better at wheeling and dealing than she, and Shirley lost.

After the election Shirley left the BSPL. She could not very well stay. She refused to become more active in the 17th A.D. Club because it was still controlled by white "bosses." She really had, as she puts it, "nowhere to go politically," and so she decided to leave politics. When she told her father of her decision, he was disappointed. When she told Conrad, he asked her if she really felt she was doing the right thing. But Shirley, for the time being at least, had had it with politics. She tried not to be bitter, and she tried to have no regrets. At times she wondered if she had made a mistake in challenging Wesley McD. Holder. But at other times she told herself she had had to make that challenge. She had been active in politics since college. She had run mimeograph machines, answered telephones, distributed leaflets, rung doorbells, written speeches, arranged rallies, spoken at rallies, led delegations. But she was not content to be a "worker" all her life. She wanted to be a leader, and she had to try. She may have lost, but she was glad she had tried.

In 1958 Shirley was still serving as director of the Hamilton-Madison House Child Care Center, but in 1959, the year after she left politics, she was offered the most important job she would have in the field of education. She accepted a position as consultant to the City Division of Day Care. She had many responsibilities. She supervised ten daycare centers, studied and evaluated the programs of many other daycare agencies, and established new centers. Shirley was happy to have the job, for she loved children, and she knew she could do a great deal for them in her new position. She and Conrad had wanted children of their own, but after two miscarriages, Shirley had decided to devote her life to the children of others. She did not need politics, she told herself; she could make her mark in the field of day care.

Shirley should have known she could not stay away from the political arena for long. Her experiences in the 17th A.D. Club and in the campaign against Wesley McD. Holder for the presidency of the BSPL may have soured her for a time. But by 1960 she was full of renewed hope that the old Democratic machine in Brooklyn could be destroyed, and full of new plans as to how she could help make that happen. In part, her new optimism was due to a general sense of hope that had touched the entire Black American community.

The civil rights movement was in full force. It had begun quietly in 1954 when the United States Supreme Court had outlawed school desegregation. It had gained momentum when a young Baptist minister named Martin Luther King led a successful Black boycott that desegregated the buses in Montgomery, Alabama. After that, King and other southern Black leaders had formed the Southern Christian Leadership Conference (SCLC) to spearhead antisegregation boycotts and demonstrations in cities across the South. Another organization, the Congress of Racial Equality (CORE), was founded by James Farmer and began staging "Freedom Rides" to desegregate interstate buses. By the late 1950s, Black college students, especially those in southern Black colleges, had been caught up in the movement. They had begun sit-ins at segregated lunch counters to force integration. In 1961 they would form their own civil rights organization, the Student Nonviolent Coordinating Committee (SNCC).

But not all Blacks were pushing for integration. While the civil rights movement was led by people such as Martin Luther King, who preached integration through nonviolent means, and was largely a southern movement, another movement was gathering strength at the same time. It was northern, city based, and rather than preaching integration it preached separatism. Rather than "love your white neighbor," it preached "hate the white devils." This was the Black Muslim movement. Founded in the 1930s in Detroit, the Black Muslim organization was basically a religious organization modeled upon but not really like the Islamic religion of Asia and Africa. It had very strict dietary and dress laws: smoking, drinking, and eating pork were prohibited; men were always to wear suits; women were to wear long dresses and to cover their heads with long scarves. Its main philosophy was that Blacks were the children of Allah (God) and that whites were the devils who had enslaved them. The Black Muslims, also known as the Nation of Islam, had grown slowly until, in the late 1940s, a young ex-convict named Malcolm Little had been converted to the religion. Changing his name to Malcolm X (all Muslims discarded their last names because they were given by white masters), this young man, who was very bright and an excellent speaker, rose quickly to an important position in the Muslim organization. When Muslim Temple Number Seven was opened in Harlem, the largest Black community in the country, Malcolm X was named its minister. Largely due to his influence, the Muslim organization grew astonishingly, although it was always a minority group among Black Americans. Malcolm X found himself the chief spokesman of the organization.

At heart Malcolm was much more of a political activist than a Muslim minister should be. It was Muslim policy not to get involved in anything outside the organization except the recruiting of new members. But Malcolm felt that the Muslims had enough power to be a great force in the American Black man's struggle for pride and dignity. He accepted interviews and speaking engagements that gave him the chance to speak out on many issues that involved American Blacks.

Shirley followed Malcolm X's career with great interest. Although she admired Martin Luther King and the other leaders of the southern-based civil rights movement, as a city Black she understood many of the things Malcolm X was saying. She did not agree with many of his antiwhite statements, but she felt that many of these statements were made for effect rather than because Malcolm really believed in them. He was trying to inspire Black pride and independence more than Black hatred of whites.

She and her father frequently discussed Malcolm X. In many ways he reminded them of Marcus Garvey. He had the ability to make Black people feel proud, feel that they could make something of themselves without the help of whites.

Thus there were many things happening in the Black community. For those who sought integration there were the leaders who preached integration through nonviolent action and there was the civil rights movement in the South. For those who wanted equal rights without, necessarily, integration, there was Malcolm X. For those, like Shirley and her father, who saw any movement for dignity in the Black community as healthy, it was a time of great hope.

Meanwhile, in Bedford-Stuyvesant, a young Black lawyer named Thomas R. Jones, a member of the Bedford-Stuyvesant Political League, decided that the BSPL had lost its effectiveness and would never regain it. What Blacks in Bedford-Stuyvesant needed, he decided, was not an independent or third party political organization, but a reform Democratic group that would challenge the machine politicians on their own ground. Other people in other parts of New York City were coming to the same decision, and Reform Democratic clubs were challenging regular clubs in many districts. When Shirley heard of Jones's plans, she could no longer stay out of politics. She wanted to get into the fight.

Thomas R. Jones. *Courtesy of AA Registry.*

She and four others who had long been active in the Brooklyn political arena joined Jones in forming the Unity Democratic Club. Then the Unity Club joined with another insurgent group, the Nostrand Democratic Club, in running a combined slate— Jones (Black, Unity) for state assemblyman and Joseph K. Rowe (white, Nostrand) for committeeman. Then came the big jobs.

They had to get the required number of voters' signatures on nominating petitions in order to have their candidates placed on the ballot. They had to get unregistered voters to register. They had to persuade registered voters that the Jones-Rowe ticket had a chance. Once again, Shirley found herself spending every free minute working on the campaign, and once again she loved it. She did not love the drudgery of speech-writing, rally-going, telephone-calling—she had been doing these things too many years to find any excitement in them. What she loved was the renewed sense of hope that machine politics in Brooklyn could be destroyed.

The machine was not destroyed that first time around. The regular Democratic Party candidates beat the Jones-Rowe ticket in the November 1961 election. But both Jones and Rowe had made a good showing, each receiving 40 percent of the total vote, and this gave the members of the Unity Club the feeling that if they kept on working, they would do better the next time. Shirley was so excited about the club's showing in the election that Conrad became excited too. Before long, he had joined the Unity Democratic Club and been assigned a district to canvass for voters.

All through 1961 they worked, signing up more members for the club, publicizing their message that Black people should represent the Black neighborhoods in Brooklyn. When it came time to select candidates for the 1962 elections, the Unity Club felt strong enough to run its own ticket: Tom Jones for both state assemblyman and district leader and Ruth Goring for district co-leader. The club also felt strong enough to adopt some very direct campaign slogans. "End Boss-Ruled Plantation Politics!" was the slogan that angered the regular Democrats most. But though the regulars branded the Unity Club campaign as "racist" and spent a great deal of money on the campaigns of their own candidates, 1962 proved to be the end for the old

Democratic machine. Both Tom Jones and Ruth Goring won first in the Democratic primary election and then in the November election. The Unity Club was now the Democratic club in Brooklyn.

"I was on the club's executive committee," Shirley recalls, "just about back where I had started my political career. That seemed a little ironic, but of course there was an enormous difference. On the old 17th A.D. Club board, it had been just a game they were playing with me and I had known it and played it for what it was worth. This time I was one of the leaders of a group that was really representative of the district, and we were in a position, for the first time, to exert some leverage on the party and the state legislature in behalf of the people who had been second-class citizens all their lives."

For the next two years the Unity Democratic Club continued its work to get more Black representation in Brooklyn politics. Although it had succeeded in ousting the old line 17th A.D. Club from power, there was still much to be done. There were, for example, only four Blacks among the twenty-two members of the Democratic county committee, a very small representation considering the large Black and Puerto Rican population in Brooklyn. The Unity Club worked for greater representation. Because there were still many, many Black and Puerto Rican residents of Brooklyn who were not registered voters, the Unity Club conducted voter registration drives to get them registered. Shirley directed or worked in all these activities, but she was discontented. She was tired of working to get other people into office. After nearly ten years in ward politics, she wanted something for herself.

"Be patient, Shirley," her father said. "I know it's hard, but you'll get your chance. If you work hard enough for what you want, you'll get it." What would she do without her father and Conrad,

Shirley sometimes wondered. They always made her feel better when she was depressed. Her father had such faith. He had worked hard all his life and was working still, but he had accomplished his main goals in life, and he was confident that his daughter could achieve her goals too.

On a hot summer morning in 1963 Charles St. Hill left his work in the yard behind the house on Prospect Place and entered the house, complaining to Ruby that he had a bad headache. He sat down on a chair and died of a general failure of his circulatory system. Shirley was at work at the City Division of Day Care when the news came by telephone. She collapsed in grief. One of the two most important people in her life was gone. Not since she had found out that the man she had first been engaged to was a criminal had she broken down so completely.

Under different circumstances her father's death might have caused her to draw closer to her mother and sisters, but Charles St. Hill's actions before his death made that impossible. He had set up a trust fund for Shirley with what was left of his savings after he had bought the house. Only the house was left to his wife and three other daughters. There has been a rift between Shirley and her family ever since.

In 1964 Shirley's chance to get something for herself in politics came. That year a seat opened up on the civil court bench in Brooklyn, and Tom Jones decided to run for it. That meant his state assembly seat would be open. Shirley Chisholm wanted that seat. She discussed the matter with her husband before she made her desire public. "It's what you want, Shirley," Conrad said. "Go out and get it." Immediately Shirley notified the Unity Democratic Club that she wanted the nomination for Tom Jones's assembly seat.

The men in the Unity Club did not have the same reaction as Conrad Chisholm had. They made it clear that they felt a woman had no business running for the State Assembly, but Shirley refused to back down. "If I had listened to all of the gentlemen around me, both Black and white, telling me, 'You know, it is best to stay in the classroom,' I wouldn't have come out here," Shirley said in a speech many years later. "But I had confidence in myself. I knew that I had ability. I knew that I could do a lot of things that some of them couldn't do and would never be able to do."

Shirley was determined to get the Unity Club nomination. She was able to convince some members simply by talking to them. Others were reminded of the things she had done for them. Still others may have come around through fear that Shirley might have "something on them." It was no secret that Conrad Chisholm was a private investigator, and Shirley used this to good advantage. Unity Club members remember hints about dossiers, or files, on people in those days. Reluctantly, the club nominated Shirley for Jones's assembly seat. Just as reluctantly the county committee accepted it. The first battle had been won. Because the Unity Democratic Club candidate was almost guaranteed to win the Democratic primary, that election was no problem. Usually the regular November election against Republican and other party candidates was no problem for the Democratic candidate either. But Shirley knew she was running with a handicap—not only was she Black, she was also a woman.

Running an election campaign costs money. Shirley knew she could not count on much help from the county organization. It never gave as much money to Black clubs as to white clubs. The Unity Club did not have much money of its own, although it could provide many eager volunteers. Mailings, leaflets, posters, the rent on halls for rallies, and all the other campaign expenses were paid for in large part by Shirley herself. Altogether, she withdrew $4,000 from the bank, a rather large chunk of her and Conrad's savings account.

However, Shirley's chief problem was not money, but being a woman in a man's game. She was not the first woman to run for the State Assembly from Brooklyn. In 1946 a Republican, Maude B. Richardson, had run and come within 200 votes of beating the Democratic candidate, a man. But the fact that another woman had once run did not make Shirley's path any easier. Many men told her outright that she should be "at home where she belonged." There were even some women who expressed the same sentiments. Although Shirley sometimes became angry—she had heard such statements against her as a woman for many years and was tired of them—she knew that anger was not the tone to take in answering these people. Instead she calmly told them that she had been serving the community for many years and that she would like the opportunity to serve on a higher level. That was how she handled those who spoke against her on an individual basis. However, in some group situations she found that the best tactic was out-talking her detractors. When speaking on street corners she was often bothered by male hecklers, but they did not bother her for long. Taking a deep breath and drawing her small body up to its full height, she would begin, "The hour is come when women will no longer be the passive recipients…." and reel off a long quote from Susan B. Anthony, her childhood suffragist heroine. By the time she finished, everyone was looking at her in amazement, and the hecklers had been stopped cold.

Conrad Chisholm also ran into some problems as he campaigned for his wife. "What kind of man are you?" people would ask. "A man who has a great little woman for a wife," he would answer. In the end, some of those who objected to Shirley's candidacy because she was a woman voted for her. In November, after a long hard campaign, Shirley won handily with 18,151 votes. Her Republican opponent, Charles Lewis, received 1,893 votes, and the Liberal candidate, Simeon Golar, 913.

A joyous victory celebration was held at Unity Democratic Club headquarters on election night. Conrad was there, as well as those members of the club who had worked hard for her. Shirley smiled so much that her cheeks began to hurt, but she could not have stopped smiling even if she had wanted to. At last she had been elected to office. At last she had some power to do things. It was one of the happiest moments of her life.

All that marred her happiness was the absence of her father. How pleased and proud he would have been to share this night with his daughter. If only he could have lived one more year to see it.

5.

ASSEMBLYWOMAN SHIRLEY CHISHOLM

Shirley Chisholm, November 1965. *Photograph by Roger Higgins, World Telegram & Sun. Courtesy of the Library of Congress.*

Shirley St. Hill Chisholm was sworn in as a New York State Assemblywoman in January 1965, but she was not the first Black woman to be elected to the Assembly. Mrs. Bessie Buchanan, the wife of a Harlem businessman, had sat in the state body several years earlier. But about all Mrs. Buchanan had accomplished was to get a certain song officially declared the New York State anthem. Shirley was determined to do much more.

As she took the oath of office with her fellow members of the Assembly, her own voice rang in her ears. She would serve the people of her district, she would serve her state, she would serve her country. While she spoke the ceremonial words, she took her own private oath: she would speak for all those who went largely unrepresented—the poor, the young, women, Black and Hispanic people. At last she was in a position where she had some real power to do so.

Bessie A. Buchanan, the first Black woman elected to the New York State assembly, ca. 1950. *Courtesy of the Schomburg Center for Research in Black Culture, Photographs and Prints Division at the New York Public Library and the New York Public Library Digital Collections.*

The very room in which she was standing held an aura of power for Shirley. The rows of green leather chairs were the seats where important decisions were made; the polished desks were the places where notes were taken, bills were drafted, fingers were tapped in deep thought. Now one of these chairs was hers, one of these desks was her work area. It had taken her a long time to get here, but at last she had made it. She had power, and she knew she had achieved that power in the right way—through the vote. Several years later she said in a speech:

> "I realized that there were only two ways to achieve creative change for Black people in this society—either politically or by open armed revolution. Malcolm X later said that very succinctly—the ballot or the bullet. Since I also believe that human life is valuable and important, I decided that for me it would have to be through the creative use of the ballot."

Now Shirley intended to make creative use of her position as assemblywoman. In the first few weeks of the Assembly session Shirley often remembered her feelings on that first day with a sigh. "I don't know how anything at all gets done around there," she told Conrad every time she arrived home in Brooklyn. It took two months for the Assembly even to elect a Speaker.

Usually the election of a Speaker in the Assembly takes only a short time. The majority party makes the decision, and it is commonly united, at least on the surface, behind one man. But in 1965 the Democratic majority in the Assembly was hopelessly split between two men, both of whom were from Brooklyn. Stanley Steingut and Anthony Travia both wanted the position and both had strong support, but neither had enough votes to win. Day after day the two sides held meetings. Night after night the two candidates sat in their rooms in the Hotel DeWitt Clinton, where Democrats stayed during the legislative session, and counted the assemblymen who visited them. Each visit could be counted as a vote. If someone Steingut counted on his side did not visit him, he sent an aide to find out why. Travia did the same thing. Shirley did not visit either Steingut or Travia, but no one went after her to ask why. She was new, she did not have influence. Besides, Tom Jones had been a friend of Steingut's. As Jones's successor Shirley was expected to follow in his footsteps.

But Shirley had a reputation for doing the unexpected, and this case was no exception. Although she was unable to do anything in terms of laws or programs during those first two months, she was able to show that she would be just as independent in state politics as she had been in Bedford-Stuyvesant politics. When one of Steingut's supporters finally mentioned the struggle to her, she informed him that she was voting for Travia.

"You'll be committing political suicide," he warned her.

But Shirley had heard that sort of warning before. She had heard it when she was appointed to the executive committee of the 17th A.D. Club and still she asked embarrassing questions. She had an idea she would hear that warning many more times in her life. "I am going to do what I believe is right," Shirley answered. She also knew she would give that answer many more times in her life.

In the end Shirley's vote did not decide the election. Those of the Republicans did. Tired of the Democrats' bickering, they settled the issue by casting all their votes for Travia. However, Shirley had let it be known that she intended to go her own way.

By the time the Assembly elected a Speaker, two months had passed, and the state legislature had not yet done any legislating! The State Senate had been ready to go to work from the start, but it could do nothing without the Assembly. It was already March. The legislative session ran only from January to April. The legislators had to get busy!

During the first two months, with the Assembly Democrats deadlocked over the choice of a Speaker, Shirley had spent more time in Brooklyn than in Albany. Every Monday morning she had taken the train or bus to Albany, and she had been able to board another train or bus to return to Brooklyn by Tuesday evening or Wednesday morning. Now, however, she spent a full five days in the capital, returning home only on weekends.

Her days were full of committee meetings and legislative sessions. Her nights were spent in her room at the Hotel DeWitt Clinton. It was at night that she felt loneliest. The men in the Assembly would go out to restaurants, movies, or bars. They did not ask Shirley to go with them. "I don't blame the fellows for not taking me out to dinner," she said a few years later. "I think there was a little fear of 'How do we handle her socially?' Men don't like independent women. Not many knew I was a regular gal. I think they were afraid to take the chance. I ate most of the time in my room. I had the TV and I read and I did my legislative homework. I went to bed early." But Shirley would have liked, once in a while, to be taken out to dinner. She would not have admitted it outright, but it came through sometimes in stiff statements like, "I do not care for the night life of the New York State Legislature."

Despite its difficulties in getting down to business, the 1965 legislative session was the most productive in many years. Shirley was appointed to the Committee on Education, and she could not have been happier with her assignment. It was "right up her alley." Many freshman assemblymen are put on committees in which they are not at all interested. It is not uncommon for a freshman from an urban area to be put on a committee dealing with rural matters. Shirley had half-expected the same thing to happen to her—as a way of punishing her for her independence in the Travia-Steingut fight. The only way she can explain why this did not happen is that she was so qualified and experienced in education that the Democratic leaders had to put her on the Committee on Education.

In the Albany state legislature, committees were as important as they were in Congress. A new bill was not simply put before the legislature, it was introduced first to the appropriate committee. A housing bill was introduced to the Housing Committee, an education bill was introduced to the Education Committee, and so on. Whether or not it ever got out of the committee and onto the floor of the Assembly depended entirely upon the committee. Very few bills introduced into committee ever reached the floor, and thus committee members had considerable power. It was up to them whether or not a bill was "reported out" to the Assembly.

Shirley introduced several education bills during that first session, and two were reported out by the Committee on Education. One provided for state aid to daycare centers. Another raised the maximum amount a local school was permitted to spend per pupil from $500 to $600, with the state paying a portion. Both these bills were passed. She also fought against some education bills introduced by others. The most important was a bill that provided state money for the purchase of textbooks by church-run schools. Shirley argued that such state aid was against the U.S. Constitution, which separated church and state. When the bill was voted on in the Assembly, 136 voted for it, and Shirley was one of 18 who voted against it. It was later passed in the State Senate and became law.

Shirley did not confine her interests to education. In her campaign for the Assembly she had promised to represent the minority groups in her district as well as the poor people. In fact her first bill to become law was one that extended unemployment insurance coverage to domestic workers.

Until Shirley's bill was made law, women who worked as maids and cooks in other people's homes could not count on a steady income. If the people they worked for moved, went on vacation, or decided they could no longer afford a maid, these domestic workers would find themselves out of work with no unemployment benefits coming in. In her speech to the Assembly Shirley talked about her own mother and the hard times the family faced when her mother lost her job and could not bring in any money. It had not been her mother's fault that the family she worked for had moved. Yet, while a secretary or factory worker could go down to the unemployment office and receive a weekly sum of money until he or she found another job, Shirley's mother could not. Shirley's bill provided that people like her now could.

The bill passed the Assembly easily. A similar bill was passed in the Senate, and Governor Nelson Rockefeller signed it into law. Shirley could be very proud of her accomplishment. She had really done something for her constituents in Bedford-Stuyvesant. Many of the women in her district were domestic workers; her bill would help them and their families greatly.

At the end of the 1965 legislative session Shirley returned to Bedford-Stuyvesant with mixed feelings. She was proud of her accomplishments, but she was frustrated over the ponderousness of the legislative process. It was a frustration that is felt by all new members of state legislatures or the national Congress. They go expecting to listen to speeches and to make speeches that will be listened to. They find out that many speeches are made to a practically empty chamber. Adam Clayton Powell wrote about his first year in the U.S. House of Representatives:

> "When one rises to make a speech after receiving a special order to do so, no one is there to listen, for the special orders come at the close of all business when weary men are returning to their homes and offices, and only the Speaker or his appointed Temporary Speaker is present. The galleries have emptied. You stand there with a document on which you have labored and you look around and no one is there to hear you except two or three members of the press. … So, when you read about an important speech on foreign policy or some other earth-shaking matter of grave concern to the nation, frequently no one has heard it."

New legislators expect to vote the way they feel is right for themselves and for their constituents. Sadly, many later change their attitudes. After she had been elected to Congress, Shirley wrote: "In Albany I first saw something I have since seen in Washington: men whose consciences urged them to one course of action were forced to take another by the political dynamics of a situation. A man might be against a bill, but one phone call from a boss, advising him that his political future rests on his being for the bill, would turn him around. I have even seen a man cry because he was not permitted to do what he knew was right."

One thing that freshmen legislators learn very soon after they take the oath of office is that there are a lot of people who are interested in how they will vote on bills. Men and women called lobbyists constantly pursue legislators and try to influence their votes. Some are from organizations such as the NAACP or from consumer groups. Others are paid by big industries. Shirley did not mind listening to lobbyists from the NAACP or other groups of which she approved, but she avoided the lobbyists from big business interests. They were always inviting her to cocktail parties, trying to take her to lunch. She was suspicious. "They're not offering all this just to be charitable," she said to herself. "They'll want something in return." She would hear rumors that such-and-such an assemblyman had voted a certain way in return for a favor.

Shirley was disappointed by her first experience in Albany, but that did not mean she was ready to give up on the American political system. "Maybe I was expecting too much," she told Conrad with a sigh. "But until we come up with something better, I'm going to stick with it."

Meanwhile the system had taken another step toward making itself very hard to like. Shirley returned home after the legislative session unable to take a much needed rest. She had to campaign for her seat in the Assembly all over again. During her stay in Albany the legislature had changed the district lines in Brooklyn.

At that time any state legislature could change the boundaries of the various state assembly districts at will. The majority would

The original political cartoon, "The Gerry-Mander," by Elkanah Tisdale. *Originally published in the Boston Centinel, 1812. Courtesy of Wikimedia Commons.*

look at a district, and if it was not made up in a way that ensured the election of people the majority wanted elected, the majority would redraw the district lines. Sometimes the resulting shapes of districts were laughable. In the 1800s in Massachusetts, a state congressman named Elbridge Gerry drew a district that looked like a horseshoe, for he knew the people in the middle would not vote the way he wanted. A Boston political cartoonist added claws and eyes to the horseshoe shape and created a salamander-like monster he called a "Gerrymander." From then on, this ridiculous kind of redistricting was called gerrymandering. Yet, although everyone knew it was wrong to draw district boundaries in this way, nothing had been done about it, and political bosses still changed the boundaries of districts at will.

Shirley was furious about the redistricting. "Now I'll have to go through another primary election in June and another regular election in November," she told Conrad. "It's ridiculous. They're just trying to harass me." But this was a case where there was no getting around the system. Shirley campaigned for the primary—and won. She campaigned for the regular election in November—and won. Whereas in the 1964 campaign she had talked about what she would do, now she was able to point to the things she had done, and in just one legislative session at that.

There was another thing she talked about in her 1965 campaign, something that meant very much to her. From the time Malcolm X had first risen to national fame, Shirley had followed his career closely, with her father at the beginning, then alone. While Malcolm had been in the Nation of Islam, better known as the Black Muslims, she had agreed with many of the things he had said about the importance of Blacks taking their destinies in their own hands. She had seen that he was much more "political" than other leaders in the Nation, and she had applauded his ability to inspire poor and hopeless Blacks. But she did not agree with many of the beliefs of the Nation, beliefs that Malcolm had preached. She did not feel preaching that whites were devils helped Black people to live in white American society. She did not feel that Blacks could successfully practice separatism within America.

Then, in 1963 Malcolm and the Nation of Islam split. He went to Mecca, the center of world Muslim religion and found that Muslims were of every race. Muslim whites and Muslim Blacks treated each other as brothers. Malcolm returned to the United States a changed man and founded his own organization. It would be a Black organization, but concerned whites would be accepted as respected co-workers. It would work toward brotherhood among Americans.

Shirley was excited about the new Malcolm. Here was a real Black leader, a man who had been born in poverty and lived a life of crime, who had uplifted himself with the help of the Black Muslims and who had finally found himself and come to understand that Blacks and whites must learn to live with each other. Other Blacks and whites were excited too, but there were some people who did not like the new Malcolm. He was a born leader, and some Blacks as well as whites considered him much more dangerous now than when he had expressed more extreme views. On February 21, 1965, Malcolm X was assassinated.

Shirley mourned his death greatly. Malcolm had been cut down just as he was approaching his real potential as a leader. She would frequently quote him in her speeches, her voice taking on a wistful quality as she remembered the greatness that might have been.

Shirley went into the November 1965 election not only with the Democratic nomination but with Liberal backing as well. She beat her Republican opponent, Fred F. Shaw, Jr., 10,508 to 2,277.

The next three years in Albany were similar to Shirley's first year except that she took the oath of office each succeeding year knowing a little more about New York State politics and how the American legislative system operates. She liked to refer to the 17th A.D. Club as her political high school and the New York State Assembly as her political college. She continued to act independently, refusing to be influenced by high-pressure lobbyists and refusing to allow her vote to be counted on by other Brooklyn Democrats just because she also happened to be a Brooklyn Democrat. Sometimes she marveled that the Democratic leaders of the Assembly did not make greater efforts to retaliate against her for her refusal to be bossed. A second redistricting forced her to run in another primary and in another regular election in 1966, but again the move was more a bother than a serious threat to her. She won the primary easily and, as the candidate of both the Democratic and Liberal parties, beat her Republican opponent, Jesse L. Vann, in November by a vote of 9,743 to 2,372.

Also, Shirley could not honestly suspect that her independence lost her votes on the bills she introduced to the Assembly.

Altogether she introduced fifty bills; eight were passed and four were signed into law, a very respectable record for two terms in the Assembly. Perhaps the bill of which Shirley was most proud was the one that created a program called SEEK (Search for Education, Elevation, and Knowledge). It was a plan to seek out deserving Black and Puerto Rican high school students and give them state scholarships to college. But SEEK was not just a financial assistance program, it was also an educational assistance program. In passing the SEEK bill, the New York state legislature recognized that the education these young men and women received in minority and ghetto schools was of poor quality than the education students in other schools received. The bill also provided for tutoring and counseling so that the scholarship students could keep up with their college work and not fall behind the other students. In its first two years of operation the SEEK program granted 8,000 scholarships to deserving minority students.

As the years in Albany passed, Shirley realized that the Democratic leadership did not control all the Democratic legislators. Many of the assemblymen disagreed with her politics, but if they agreed with her that a particular law was needed, they would vote for her bill. Even when they disagreed with her, they did so because of their own beliefs, not because of any resentment of her. Shirley recalls that one assemblyman said to her, "You know, Chisholm, I think you're wrong; but you're sincere, I've got to give you that." Shirley would have done what she thought was right, whatever the consequences. But it pleased her that she had earned the sometimes grudging respect of her colleagues in Albany.

Shirley Chisholm had succeeded. She proved that a Black woman could make it in Albany. Although she had not been the first Black woman to serve there, she had been the first to make a meaningful contribution. Back home in Bedford-Stuyvesant, most of the men who had suggested four years before that she stay at home where she belonged had come to respect and support her. And most of the women were fiercely behind her. Shirley knew she had a real power base in Bedford-Stuyvesant, and by the end of 1967 she knew exactly how she was going to use it.

Three years earlier, in 1964, the U.S. Supreme Court, in its "one man, one vote" ruling, provided that the voting population in each congressional or assembly district should be approximately equal to the voting population of every other district. This forced many states and local areas to redistrict, or redraw voting district lines. However, the Supreme Court ruling was not so detailed that all districts had to be redrawn to achieve exact equality. Loop holes still existed, but they were harder to find; and this was fortunate for Black people in many areas.

In 1967 the New York state legislature set up a committee to redraw some of the Brooklyn district lines. This committee could have drawn the lines so that Bedford-Stuyvesant would be split, each piece being combined with predominantly white districts outside the area. However, the growing Black population of Brooklyn was concentrated in the Bedford-Stuyvesant section. It was time for them to have a Black representative in Congress, so the committee created a new congressional district, the twelfth.

When the Black people of Bedford-Stuyvesant heard about the new 12th C.D., they were excited. At last they would have a representative in Congress. Adam Clayton Powell had tried to speak for them, as well as for all Black people around the country, but he was, after all, from Harlem. Now they would have their own voice in Congress.

There was much speculation about who would make a try for the seat in the June 1968 primaries. City Councilman William

C. Thompson, a former state senator, the Reverend Milton Galamison, an NAACP leader, and Mrs. Dolly Robinson, a labor organizer, were all very interested in running. So was Shirley Chisholm.

Shirley knew from long experience that just wanting something was not enough. One had to plan for it and work for it. "Before I make a move, I analyze everything," she often reminds her listeners.

Even before she and Conrad talked seriously about her running, she had done some homework. She had obtained copies of the election rolls and some census statistics, and she had studied the population of the new district carefully. She knew that the majority of the people in the district were Black, but she found there were a number of Italians in the part of the Bushwick section that the district encompassed and many Jews in the Crown Heights section. There were also many Hispanics in the Williamsburg section. These voters would have to be taken into account by any candidate.

Closer study of the election rolls revealed something about the district that was very important to Shirley. There seemed to be thousands more women voters than men, between 10,000 and 13,000 more, she later figured. Meanwhile the others who were thinking of making a try for the congressional seat had not thought to look at the population of the district in terms of how many men and women voters were in it. Shirley had an edge on them already.

As the new year approached and speculation about who would run for the seat increased, a Democratic citizens' committee formed itself in the district and announced that it would choose the Democratic nominee. When the new 12th C.D. had been formed, the King's County Democratic Committee had pledged that it would not choose the nominee but would leave the matter "up to the people." This announcement was greeted in the district with suspicion: since when did a county machine volunteer not to become involved in any aspect of county politics? The citizens' committee intended to call the machine's bluff. Its chief purpose was to prevent the nomination of a candidate whom the machine would support, a candidate who would take orders from the county leaders instead of doing what was best for the people of the district.

The citizens' committee invited many of the potential candidates to come for interviews. Shirley, the only woman they invited, had a long interview. Some of the things they expected from a candidate were unrealistic, she told them. Some of their demands for the district just would not be possible. She told them what kind of candidate she would be and what kinds of things she would try to do if she were elected. But she was far from confident when the interview was over.

"I don't know," she sighed to Conrad as he helped her off with her coat. "I tried to put it to them straight. I hope they don't choose someone who went in there and yessed them all through the interview."

A few days later the citizens' committee announced its choice— Shirley Chisholm, by unanimous vote. Shirley was surprised and pleased. Later she learned that she was the only potential candidate who had disagreed with the committee, and that was why they had picked her.

As Shirley had expected, the county organization broke its promise not to meddle in the choice of nominee. Although the county leaders never made an official endorsement, their every action made clear that they favored William C. Thompson. When they met with the eight leaders of the four assembly districts within the 12th C.D. to pick a candidate, the choice was Thompson. Shirley got only two votes, and one of those was her own.

The decision did not mean that Shirley could not run. As long as she got enough signatures on her nominating petition, she could enter the Democratic primary. The decision did mean that she would not get any financial help from the county organization nor would she get any campaign help from the district leaders. The primary campaign would be a three-way fight among Thompson, Dolly Robinson, and Shirley Chisholm. Shirley began the fight with only her own Fifty-Fifth Assembly District, the Unity Democratic Club—"and the people," Shirley always adds—on her side.

Then, out of the blue, came a surprising and welcome telephone call. It was Wesley McD. Holder. Nearly ten years had passed since the two had struggled for leadership of the Bedford-Stuyvesant Political League and Shirley had lost. They had bumped into each other from time to time, but the barrier between them had remained as solid as ever. Shirley never expected to receive a call from Mac, and she was flabbergasted when she did.

Holder had decided to put the past behind him and put goals ahead of personalities. He had often said he hoped to live long enough to elect a Black congressman. Now he was in his early seventies, and he saw a chance for Shirley, provided that he organized her campaign. He knew that although there were more nonwhites than whites in the district, the number of registered white voters was greater. To win, Shirley would have to get almost every nonwhite vote plus some white votes.

"You can't win without me and the people in the street," Holder told Shirley. "I'll help you get to them." Shirley accepted, and after nearly ten years the two renewed their political partnership. In the months that followed, they also renewed their friendship.

They worked nineteen hours a day. Mac arranged meetings and speaking engagements, called on old political and community friends for support, looked for campaign contribution sources.

Together they plotted strategy. "Everyone in the Fifty-fifth Assembly District knows you already, Shirley," Mac said. "You have to concentrate on those neighborhoods where you are not so well known. Appeal to the women to help you; they're your strongest power base."

"We need a slogan," Shirley suggested, "something catchy, but meaningful too. I'm a fighter; nobody has ever bought me or bossed me. How about: 'Fighting Shirley Chisholm—Unbought and Unbossed'?"

The People's Choice flyer advocating for Chisholm's election, 1968.
Courtesy of the Gotham Center.

Posters, bumperstickers, shopping bags bearing the slogan were printed and distributed. Every neighborhood woman leader was contacted and asked to help. "Bring your women in," Shirley told them. They held raffles and bake sales to raise money. They held teas and barbecues at which she was the guest of honor. They handed out Shirley Chisholm campaign literature and made endless telephone calls. They did all that Brooklyn women interested in politics had traditionally done, but this time was different. This time they were not doing "women's work" for a male candidate; they were doing necessary work for a female candidate. And if they were successful, they would have helped elect the first Black woman ever to serve in the House of Representatives.

Shirley encountered sexist prejudice in this campaign, just as she had in her campaign for the assembly seat. But this time she did not have to silence hecklers with a long quote from Susan B. Anthony. She could reel off an equally long list of her qualifications and accomplishments. She could have added that she was working harder for the nomination than any of her opponents. William Thompson felt so confident that he took a vacation right in the middle of the primary campaign.

Not Shirley. Every night she was at someone's home, at some party, at some shopping center campaigning. Every weekend she organized a motorcade decorated with campaign signs and complete with sound truck. They covered every part of the district. She smiled until her cheeks hurt and made speeches until she was hoarse. She drove herself so hard that Conrad worried about her. "You've got a good chance of winning," he said, "but if you don't slow down the people will have a congresswoman with a hospital bed for an office." But Shirley kept at her grueling pace. A U.S. congressional seat—she knew she had a good chance at it, and she was going to go all out for it.

Sometimes she marveled at how far Black people had come in only about twenty years. Thanks to people such as Thurgood Marshall and other Black lawyers and to organizations such as the NAACP, most of the racist laws had been struck down. Adam Clayton Powell and others also had helped pass laws that would provide equal opportunity for Black people. Martin Luther King and other leaders of the civil rights movement had ended segregation in many areas across the South. Groups like the Student Nonviolent Coordinating Committee had conducted voter registration drives to sign up Black voters in the South. Blacks were running for state and local offices, and that very year several were running for mayor. Martin Luther King was now bringing his campaign for equality north and urging Black hospital and sanitation workers to unite for higher wages and better benefits. And a Black woman was running for a congressional seat from Brooklyn. Things were really looking up for Black people.

Then in April Shirley and all Black people, as well as many whites across the country, were plunged into despair. Dr. Martin Luther King was assassinated. For many he had been the "King of Love," and the fact that he had been assassinated brought many Black people back to the sobering reality that although they had made some gains, racism was still rampant in the country. In cities across the nation, Blacks rioted in grief and despair, but in New York the Black neighborhoods expressed their grief in a quieter manner. The people listened to their community leaders, who told them rioting would do no good. "Martin would not have wanted us to give up," Shirley told her audiences. "He knew his life was in danger. He told us he knew. He told us he might not get to the other side of the mountain with us, but he wanted us to keep on without him."

It was a sad time for Black people, those spring months of 1968. First Martin Luther King and then in June, just after the California presidential primary, Robert F. Kennedy was also assassinated. Like his brother President John F. Kennedy, Robert Kennedy had been popular in the Black community, especially Bedford-Stuyvesant, in which the junior senator from New York had taken a particular interest. He had announced his candidacy for the

Democratic presidential nomination, which would be decided at the Democratic National Convention in Chicago in August. When he was killed in California he was actively campaigning.

Shirley had liked many of the things Kennedy had to say, but she had resented the fact that he had not come out in support of her bid for the Democratic nomination for the 12th C.D. seat. Wesley reminded her that it would be unwise for Kennedy to get involved in local politics, but Shirley remained unconvinced. When she heard that he had been assassinated, she remembered her resentment and regretted it.

Like other Black people, Shirley felt a tremendous sense of loss over the deaths of King and Kennedy. She felt more alone and more despairing. She also began to worry about how the assassinations would affect her chances and those of other Blacks running for political office that year. How will these events affect the Black vote? she wondered. Black people are still so suspicious of the system, still so unsure that voting and electing their own representatives will do any good. What if in their despair they give up?

On primary day the voter turnout was small. Watching the returns from Black districts, Shirley knew she'd had cause to worry. She wished those voters who had not cast their ballots had felt more hope, but she really could not blame them. She herself did not lose hope, however. After all, she had tried to reach all the people in the district, the Jews, the Italians, and the Hispanics as well as the Blacks. Apparently she had succeeded.

Although the voter turnout was small, it was enough to elect Shirley Chisholm. With 5,686 votes she won by about 1,000 over William Thompson, who received 4,907. Dolly Robinson, who came in third with 1,848, took votes away from Thompson, not from Shirley. Shirley carried all four white sections in the district.

James Farmer, 1963. Photograph by Walter Albertin. *Courtesy of the Library of Congress.*

Her fight was far from over. Usually the winner of the Democratic primary was practically assured of victory in the November election because Brooklyn was heavily Democratic. But this year the Republicans were going all out to win the new congressional district seat. They had brought in James Farmer to be their candidate.

Farmer's name was well known in the Brooklyn Black community, as well as in the rest of the country. In the 1950s he had helped to found the Congress of Racial Equality, which began a series of Freedom Rides to desegregate interstate buses. Farmer had also been active in all the boycotts and demonstrations that CORE had staged. He had been shot at and arrested and jailed. During the civil rights movement, he became a major hero. Very few Black voters had not heard of him.

When it was announced that Farmer had received the Republican and Liberal endorsements for the 12th C.D. seat, Shirley was furious. "He doesn't even live in Brooklyn," she protested. "Why doesn't he run for something in Harlem?" Mac reminded her that it wasn't necessary for a congressman to live in the district he represented and that Farmer had rented an apartment on Herkimer Street near Nostrand Avenue for appearance's sake.

"He will be a formidable opponent, Shirley," said Mac. "He has a name. He'll play up the whole male thing. But, as you found out, there are over 10,000 more women in the district. If we work hard, we'll beat him."

No sooner was the primary over than Shirley started campaigning for the November election. Again posters and pamphlets and shopping bags were run off and distributed. But Farmer got national television coverage, which was worth a lot more. Sometimes, it seemed to Shirley, she could hardly turn on the nightly television news without seeing James Farmer campaigning for the 12th C.D. seat. "This is unfair," she cried, and began calling the local television stations to ask why both candidates for the election were not covered. One man she reached put it to her straight. "Who are you?" he asked. "A little schoolteacher who happened to go to the Assembly."

Every weekend Shirley got her motorcades moving and mounted sound trucks to plead her cause and ask the people to vote for her. But time after time her voice was drowned out when they met one of Farmer's motorcades. His sound trucks were manned by young Blacks with Afro hairstyles, dressed in dashikis, beating tom-toms. Farmer was going all out to project a male image to contrast with her femininity. The television reporters were attracted in droves and swarmed after Farmer, while Shirley, frustrated, was left alone.

She began to despair. "How can I compete against a candidate who is nationally known and who has all that money?" she asked Conrad.

"By appealing to the people," he answered.

"But how do I know the people won't go with Farmer?" she insisted. Shortly after the primary she received her answer.

One evening when Shirley and Conrad were at home enjoying a rare time of relaxation, the doorbell suddenly rang. Shirley went to answer it, wondering who it could be. A woman was standing on the steps. In the light of the front-door lantern Shirley could see that she was poorly dressed. The woman pushed an envelope into Shirley's hand.

"This is the first, Chisholm," she said.

"Wait a minute," Shirley exclaimed in disbelief. "There's money in this envelope!"

The envelope contained $9.69 in bills and coins. Shirley learned that it had been collected from people on welfare at a bingo party. Poor people wanted her to win, and they were contributing what little they could to help her.

After the woman left, Shirley sat down and cried. Her despair was gone, her hope renewed.

If Shirley had worked hard for previous elections, she worked doubly hard now. She knew it was the only way to counter the money the Farmer campaign could spend and the press coverage his campaign was receiving. All through July and into August she worked, and then, suddenly, she was told she could not work at all.

Even before the primary election, Shirley had known something was wrong, but she had refused to admit it. She would not let anything, even her health, get in the way of her primary bid. After the primary she had started to work just as hard for the regular election, but those around her saw how tired she looked. Conrad insisted that she see a doctor.

"But I have meetings. I have places to speak. I can't possibly see a doctor until after November," Shirley had protested. Conrad stood firm. Shirley went to a doctor.

She found, to her fear and dismay, that a tumor had been growing inside her pelvic area for two years. The tumor was not malignant, the doctor assured her, it was not cancerous, but it had to be operated on right away.

"Can't it wait until after the election?" Shirley pleaded. "I've had it for two years; a few months more can't matter."

"We must operate now," the doctors insisted.

So Shirley reluctantly left her campaign to Wesley McD. Holder and her other supporters and entered a hospital to have her operation. She knew that James Farmer would continue to tour the district with his tom-tom-beating Black male campaigners; he would continue to receive extensive publicity. Shirley was not one to give up easily, but as she waited in the hospital for her operation, she wondered how she would ever win the November election.

Shirley did not mind the operation. It was the convalescing after she returned home in August that drove her crazy. "All I do is stay in bed or sit in a chair all day," she complained to Conrad. "I've got to get out and speak to the people."

Conrad said no. Her doctor said no. But Shirley said, "The stitches aren't in my mouth. I'm going out."

Once more, she rode on the sound trucks and arrived at shopping centers to announce, "This is Fighting Shirley Chisholm. I'm back and I'm fine." Again, Shirley could not do as much campaigning as she would have liked. This time it was not illness that interrupted her campaign, but politics.

It was August, the month of the Democratic National Convention in Chicago. Shirley was intensely interested in the convention, where the Democratic presidential nominee would be chosen, but she did not feel she was up to attending. Then in late August she received a call from Thomas Fortune, a Brooklyn leader who had consistently backed her. New York Democrats, he informed her, wanted to elect her Democratic National Committeewoman from New York, a high honor.

Shirley could not refuse. Despite the fact that she still needed rest, despite the fact that Farmer's campaign was still going strong, Shirley went off to Chicago to attend the most infamous Democratic convention in history. From beginning to end it was plagued by violence. Groups of poor people, young people against the Vietnam War, women and Blacks demanding a greater voice in the political process protested in the streets outside the convention hall. While police beat the protesters back, the convention delegates tried to conduct their business. But it was difficult to do so when many of the very people they were supposed to represent were so clearly demonstrating that they did not feel represented at all.

On the last day of the convention Hubert H. Humphrey and Edmund S. Muskie were nominated as the Democratic candidates for president and vice-president. They would face the Republican candidates Richard M. Nixon and Spiro T. Agnew. Flying back to New York, Shirley did not feel very hopeful about the Democrats' chances of winning. The violence in Chicago would be associated in the public mind with the Democrats, and that would be hard for the party's candidates for national, state, and local offices to overcome. She wondered how much it would affect her race with James Farmer. It was not a pleasant thought. Shirley returned to Brooklyn to find that Farmer had been very busy during her absence. He was directing his entire campaign toward the difference in their sexes. Shirley Chisholm was a nice woman who meant well, but the 12th C.D. needed a man. He had known about her operation and about her going to Chicago, but he acted as if she had been absent from the campaign because she knew she was no match for him. Shirley realized she would have to work very hard in the remaining months of the campaign.

She had two "cards up her sleeve" and decided to use them. She had relied on the support of women's groups before, but now she appealed to them for help not on the basis of a straightforward "I am the candidate who can do the best job" but on Farmer's terms: "I am a woman and you are women, and let's show Farmer that woman-power can beat him." The response was fantastic.

"The women are fierce about Shirley," said Conrad. "She can pick up the phone and call two hundred women and they'll be here in an hour. And she gives them nothing more than a 'thank you' and a buffet supper."

Her other "card" was her ability to speak Spanish. She had minored in Spanish during college, and her work with daycare centers in Spanish-speaking areas had helped her keep her fluency in the language. This meant a great deal to the people in the Hispanic sections of the new 12th C.D. In fact she was more sure of carrying these sections than the Black neighborhoods.

Shirley did not rely only on her appeal to women as a woman and her fluency in Spanish. She knew that a successful campaign meant hard work and "getting to the people." She continued to spend hours and hours riding around in a sound truck. The truck would pull up to a housing project and she would get on top of the truck and announce, "Ladies and Gentlemen of the Brevoort Houses, this is Fighting Shirley Chisholm coming through."

There were always many people out on the grounds and surrounding streets of the projects. But she would draw many more out; windows would slide up and heads and shoulders would appear as people leaned out to hear better. She would catch their interest with a joke or strong word image: "They call me Fighting Shirley Chisholm. My mother tells me I was born fighting. She says I was kicking so hard in the womb she knew I was aching to get out and fight."

Once she had attracted an audience she spoke about her accomplishments as a state assemblywoman and about what she hoped to do as a congresswoman. She criticized Farmer as a kind of carpet-bagger—an outsider who did not really care about the people of the district and who would use the congressional seat not to help the people but for his own personal gain. Audiences of women were asked to show woman-power. Mixed audiences were asked to look past the candidates' sex and focus on who could do the best job.

Shirley and Farmer had several public debates. To this day each believes he or she outshone the other. Farmer has a great presence on stage or off. Shirley, small and bespectacled, does look more like a schoolteacher than a politician. Yet when she mounts a platform, something happens; she appears taller than she is and her voice is commanding. Furthermore, Shirley, who had lived in Bedford-Stuyvesant most of her life, plainly had a better idea of the needs and issues directly affecting the area than Farmer had.

It was not just her call for woman-power, or her fluency in Spanish, or her accomplishments as an assemblywoman, or her speaking ability, or Farmer's status as a stranger to Brooklyn that won the election for Shirley. It was a combination of all these factors, plus a fine campaign manager and lots of hard work. The victory was a wonderful vindication of Shirley's ideas, accomplishments, and efforts. In the November election she outpolled Farmer 2.5 to 1. Although he ran on both the Republican and Liberal lines, Farmer received only 13,777 votes. The Conservative candidate, Ralph J. Carrane, got 3,771.

And Shirley got a whopping 34,885 votes. Brooklyn's new Twelfth Congressional District would provide the House of Representatives with its first Black female member.

Shirley took off for a much needed three-week vacation in Jamaica.

Shirley Chisholm shortly after her ground-breaking election to Congress, surrounded by her campaign team, 1968. *Courtesy of AP Images.*

6.

CONGRESSWOMAN SHIRLEY CHISHOLM

From the moment she arrived in Washington, Shirley started doing things that were not usually done by a legislator. In the first place she entered the House chambers, where the oath-taking ceremonies were taking place, with her coat and hat on. She was late. Many of her friends and relatives had come to Washington to see her sworn in only to find that there was no room for them in the galleries. She had tried to use her influence to get them seated, but she was unsuccessful. (This was her first lesson in the lack of power of a freshman legislator.) By the time she reached the House chamber, she thought it was more important to get right to her seat than to waste time hanging up her coat and hat in the House cloakroom. But before she could take her seat, she was told she was breaking a house rule: no representative ever took his seat in his hat and coat. A little embarrassed, Shirley had to hurry back to the cloakroom and return to take her oath of office.

Of course she was breaking precedent merely by being who and what she was. Anyone scanning the House floor could see that. There were a few women—there, there, and there. There were a few Blacks—there, there, and there. There was only one Black congresswoman: Shirley Chisholm. Dwarfed by the men who flanked her, Shirley stood ramrod straight and held her right hand up to take the oath. The others, spectators and legislators alike, were aware of her presence, and Shirley was aware of the meaning of her presence. No one, not even Shirley, could foresee the attention she would later command. For the time being she was simply a "first."

Next Shirley broke an unwritten rule that freshman congressmen should not talk to important men such as House Speaker John McCormack. She knew how much her friends and family had looked forward to seeing her sworn in, and she had wanted very much to have them see the ceremony. Then she had a great idea. Why not have a private swearing-in ceremony at her hotel? She called Speaker McCormack—would he administer the oath of office to her a second time? Graciously McCormack accepted the invitation, but fellow representatives gossiped about Shirley's nerve.

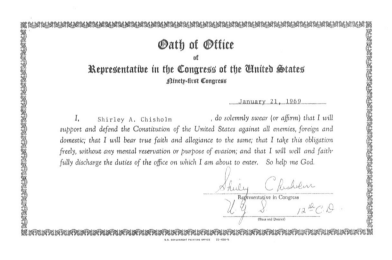

Shirley Chisholm's Oath of Office, 1969. *Courtesy of the National Archives Museum.*

"You have to have nerve," Shirley told Conrad and Mac during her first visit to Brooklyn after being sworn into office. "You have to have nerve even to get around. I feel like I did the first day I went to P.S. 84. There seemed to be so many floors and so

Shirley Chisholm taking her Oath of Office, 1969.
Courtesy of BOTWC.

many halls. At least there weren't any tunnels at P.S. 84. I have to deal with so many elevators and escalators and tunnels and passageways. I'm lucky that there are so many Black people working there as elevator operators and guards. I think they make a special effort to help me find my way around because I'm one of them.

"And once I get to the House chambers," she continued, "there is another maze waiting—a maze of minds and loyalties and compromises and bargains. You wouldn't believe what goes on there. I tried to explain the situation in Albany to you when I was there. The situation in Congress is worse, I can tell, but I can't explain it to you until I understand it myself."

Shirley Chisholm can size up a situation or a person in the time it takes to snap one's fingers. She may not immediately know the reason for her reaction, but she can make the decision— and further observation and experience usually prove her first impression correct. Before she had even come to understand fully the workings of Congress, she had found those workings suspect and had decided not to conform to them.

Shortly thereafter she committed the most serious breach of commonly accepted conduct for a freshman representative: she dared to protest her committee assignment. As in the New York state legislature, House committees are very important. They decide which bills reach the floor of the House and, thus, which bills have even a chance of being passed.

Committee assignments, like so many other things in Congress, depend upon seniority. The longer legislators have served in Congress, the better their chances of getting an assignment they want. Thus, although freshman members can list in order of preference the committees they would like to be on, they rarely get their choices. Shirley wanted most to be on the Education and Labor Committee. Her second choice was the Banking and Currency Committee. After that, she requested the Post Office and Civil Service Committee or the Government Operations Committee. She felt her twenty years' experience in education qualified her for the Education and Labor Committee and felt she could be a real asset to the committee. But she would have been satisfied with even her fourth choice.

To her dismay Shirley was not assigned to any of her committee choices. Instead she was appointed to the Agriculture Committee and to the subcommittees of rural development and forestry under that committee. "Can you imagine that?" Shirley asked Conrad when she called to tell him the news. "No assignment could be less relevant to my background or to the needs of the predominantly Black and Puerto Rican people who elected me. I don't care if freshman congressmen are supposed to be seen and not heard—I'm going to fight this."

Once again Shirley went against custom and called Speaker McCormack. At first he advised her to "be a good soldier."

"I've been a good soldier long enough," Shirley explained. If McCormack did not help her, she warned, she would have to take steps to help herself. McCormack did not like to be threatened, but he knew Shirley's reputation; she wasn't just making idle threats. He agreed to speak with Wilbur Mills, chairman of the

House Ways and Means Committee and one of the most powerful Democrats in the House.

Mills was not at all happy about Shirley's threat of rebellion, and he hinted at his feelings when he encountered her for the first time shortly afterward. Shirley is a great mimic, but one of her best impressions is of Wilbur Mills at this meeting: "Er-ah, Missus Chisholm," she says, pushing her voice down as deep as she can and using

Congressman Wilbur Mills, 1971. Photograph by Warren K. Leffler. *Courtesy of the Library of Congress.*

an Arkansas drawl, "we, er-ah, want to welcome you, er-ah, to the Congress, but, my-my-my-my-my-my, Missus Chisholm, we certainly hope you, er-ah, not gonna turn evahthing up side-down heah."

But Shirley was willing to turn things upside-down to change her committee assignment. On the floor of the House she tried to make a motion to this effect. But the Speaker is the one who recognizes or allows members of the House to speak, and Speaker McCormack refused to recognize Shirley. Stubbornly she continued to rise, showing that she wanted to speak. Pretty soon the other members were whispering and chuckling.

Finally Shirley left her seat and marched right down to the well of the chamber in front of the Speaker's lectern. Speaker McCormack leaned over the dais and looked down at the determined little figure. The rest of the House tittered and chuckled. There was nothing McCormack could do but recognize the freshman congresswoman. Shirley protested her committee assignment vigorously. There were only nine Black members in the House, she said, and if Black people in this country were represented in proportion to their numbers there should have been more than forty (actually, she realized later, she should have said fifty-five). Since Black people were not represented in proportion to their numbers in Congress, Congress should at least see to it that the few representatives Black people had were placed in positions in which they could do some good.

An assignment to a committee on forestry certainly was not one of them.

Shirley's resolution that she be taken off the Agriculture Committee and offered another committee assignment was accepted. Shirley felt that she had won an important victory.

Fellow representatives disagreed. "They'll never forgive you for this," they said. Once again she was warned, "You're committing political suicide." "That phrase sort of made me feel at home," Shirley would later recall.

She listened more closely, however, to another congressman when he urged her to think twice before taking on the whole Congress in her fight for what she wanted. This congressman was Adam Clayton Powell, who had long experience trying to be independent in the House of Representatives. He was at the 1969 congressional session after an absence of nearly two years, for in 1967 the House had voted to bar him from his congressional seat because of "misconduct."

Throughout his congressional career Powell had been plagued by attempts to discredit him, both by Congress and by other branches of the U.S. government. His income tax returns had been audited and he had spent many years in the courts before he had been found innocent of tax fraud. A trip to Europe on congressional business on which he had been accompanied by two young female secretaries had been criticized as a "shameless junket," even though many other congressmen took large staffs and sometimes their families along on government-paid trips.

Adam Clayton Powell was no saint. He probably deserved some of the trouble that hounded him. But even his strongest critics had to admit that in many cases it was obvious that Adam was being punished not for a particular instance of misconduct but for being such an outspoken critic of white society. Aging and tired now, he wanted to warn the new congresswoman.

"You're a very outspoken person," he told Shirley. "They'll gang up on you. So long as you're quiet, you'll get along. But you're not." Shirley listened respectfully to what Adam had to say, but she did not see herself following in his footsteps. "They won't get me because I'm going to be very careful," she told him with assurance. It surprised a lot of people when Shirley was given another committee assignment and was not punished politically for her defiance. She was assigned to the Veterans' Affairs Committee, and while it was still not an assignment she would have picked herself, it was better than her first assignment. As she told people, "There are a lot more veterans in my district than there are trees."

Like Adam Clayton Powell in previous years, Shirley continued to defy the rules by being outspoken on the floor of the House. Her fight for a change of committee assignment was followed by her announcement of her intention to vote No on every bill that came before the House which provided funds for the Department of Defense. At that time the Vietnam War was still in full force, as was the antiwar movement in the United States. Shirley had not made the war a central issue in her campaign.

She had been more concerned with issues that affected the daily lives of the people in her district and of poor people everywhere: housing, jobs, education, discrimination. Richard Nixon, who had been elected president in 1968 and had taken his oath of office in the same month that Shirley had taken the congressional oath, made the ending of the war one of his main issues. Though Shirley did not share the president's views on many issues, she did feel optimistic that he would make every effort to end the war. But as the months wore on, it seemed to Shirley that what the Administration was doing was continuing the war and slowing up efforts in areas of social action.

"When President Nixon announced … he had decided that the United States would not be safe until we started to build an ABM [antiballistic missile] system, and that the Head Start program in the District of Columbia was to be cut back for lack of money, that was enough for me," Shirley recalls. "I started working on my maiden speech, my first in the House. For whatever it would be worth, even if it would only get it off my chest, I had to tell the world that it was wrong to plan to spend billions on an elaborate and unnecessary weapons system when disadvantaged children were getting nothing."

It was in her maiden speech in the House, that she vowed to vote against any defense spending bills. In a way it was kind of a negative approach to her job as a legislator, but it was a practical approach. As she said, "The business of the House goes on with or without [the freshman congressman]." The only clout she had was her ability to vote No.

Shirley had wasted no time in making herself known on Capitol Hill, but if her supporters thought her display of independence about committee assignments would be followed by the introduction of ambitious and forward-looking bills, they were being unrealistic.

Shirley herself was quite realistic. In Albany she had been impressed with the rows of green leather chairs and the long polished wooden desks in front of them. She had found, though, that an impressive room does not mean that impressive things are done in that room. The House chamber with three times as many desks and chairs was much more impressive than the Albany Assembly, but this time Shirley was not awed. When she had taken the oath of office in Congress, she had not spoken the ceremonial words with the same idealism as in 1965.

By now Shirley knew the political rules. She had worked her way up through Brooklyn politics and she had served two terms in the New York state legislature. There she had started at the bottom of the ladder and worked her way up to the top. Now, as a freshman congresswoman, she was once again at the bottom of a ladder, the congressional ladder of seniority. Only with seniority could a legislator hope to get bills passed.

As she once put it: "Even if he is not Black and not a member of the smallest faction in the House, the left-liberal one, a freshman member is not going to get many—if any—laws passed. He has no clout. No one cares what he does; the business of the House goes on with or without him." Shirley's lack of belief in her ability to do much in the way of lawmaking was reflected in her attendance record at congressional sessions during her first term: 55 percent.

What Shirley did do as a congresswoman was try to help the people in her district and other poor people in more direct ways. She established well-staffed offices in both Washington, D.C., and Brooklyn, where Mac Holder was in charge. To these offices individuals came with requests for help in getting jobs, in fighting discrimination in housing, in fighting unjust imprisonment. Local social agencies asked for help in securing federal grants or in saving existing programs. Shirley spent hours every week in both offices. Every Friday night she sat in a large back room in the district office and listened to the problems of her constituents.

The people of the 12th C.D. knew they could come to her no matter what their problem. Whether they were trying to get into a low-income housing project or a job-training program, whether they wanted a street light installed on their block or more police patrols, they knew that a letter or a call from a congresswoman could solve many of these problems, and Shirley willingly used her power in this way.

The District of Columbia was represented in Congress by only one nonvoting delegate, Walter Fauntroy. The poor people and the minority-group citizens of Washington, D.C., needed more than that, and Shirley could not refuse their requests for help. Within a short time Shirley found herself not only congresswoman from Brooklyn's 12th C.D. but the adopted congresswoman for the Black population of Washington, D.C. Some people in Brooklyn criticized her for paying so much attention to the District of Columbia, but Shirley answered, "I did not seek out D.C.—D.C. almost drove me 'nuts' when I came here. What is one who is committed to the underdog to do when help is being sought?" Besides, she knew that she would have the support of many of the residents of Washington, D.C., if she ever needed it.

Shirley also maintained a heavy speaking schedule. Her maiden speech in Congress, in which she expressed her strongest antiwar feelings, caused her to be in great demand on the nation's college campuses, the heart of the antiwar movement. Because she was the first Black congresswoman, she was also sought after by the fast-growing women's liberation groups.

She was criticized for accepting so many speaking invitations. Some critics felt she should spend more time as a congresswoman and less time on the lecture circuit. Others felt she was spending too much time talking to white college students and not enough time talking to Blacks. Shirley reminded her critics that she had spent a lot of her own money on her congressional campaign and was using her speaker's fees to pay off debts. She also pointed out that the best way to get support for an issue, whether it was an antiwar stand or a plea to end discrimination, was to take that case to the people.

In addition, Shirley was criticized for her support of the women's liberation movement, and by September 1969 she was faced with a critical decision: whether or not to publicly support abortion, one of the most important issues of that movement. In August she was asked to be president of the National Association for the Repeal of Abortion Laws (NARAL).

NARAL celebrates their 50th anniversary with an image of Shirley Chisholm as she addresses the crowd at a 1972 rally for abortion rights. *Courtesy of NARAL.*

Whether or not to accept the position was a difficult decision for Shirley to make. There were many arguments against accepting and only one, really, for it. Shirley realized that in accepting the presidency of the NARAL, she would be publicly aligning herself with the women's liberation movement. Although the movement claimed to represent all women, its active members were chiefly white, middle-class women. She also realized that many Blacks saw the abortion issue in racial terms. Some pointed out that the birth rate of Blacks—and of poor people in general—is considerably higher than that of middle-class whites. They felt that there was power in these numbers and that abortion was a "plot" to reduce this power. The label these Blacks used for this was genocide, the killing of a race. Finally, the abortion issue was not at that time a politically practical issue for any legislator, Black or white, to support.

The argument for Shirley to accept the position came from her own conscience. In the past, she had not been in favor of repealing all abortion laws. In Albany she had fought for the passage of laws that would have made abortion readily available, but only to those who she then believed really should have it—victims of rape, for example, or women whose lives were endangered by pregnancy. Since then, however, she had known several women whose lives had been endangered by illegal abortions performed improperly or under unhygienic conditions. She knew that people with money were able to pay the fees of good medical doctors, while the poor usually had to resort to quacks. She had also come to believe that abortion should be the decision of the individual, not of the government. If her critics chose to see her support of abortion as support of women's liberation, that was their problem, not hers. If her colleagues in the House decided their own positions on the issue in terms of political expediency, that was their problem. She had rarely supported or fought against an issue because it was politically wise.

The genocide charge did bother her. After all, she was Black, and the feelings of the Black community were important to her. However, she saw through the genocide charge:

"To label family planning and legal abortion programs 'genocide' is male rhetoric, for male ears. It falls flat to female listeners, and to thoughtful male ones. Women know, and so do many men, that two or three children who are wanted, prepared for, reared amid love and stability, and educated to the limit of their ability will mean more for the future of the Black and brown races from which they come than any number of neglected, hungry, ill-housed and ill-clothed youngsters."

In the end, after a great deal of thought, Shirley made her decision. She would agree to become honorary president of NARAL. Though she would be criticized for compromising, for accepting and not accepting the position at the same time, she would have no trouble defending her decision. "I am a congresswoman," she said. "I have responsibilities to the people in my district and to poor people and people who are victims of inequality everywhere. If I accepted the presidency of the NARAL, I would not be able to devote the time to it that I would like. As honorary president, I will do all I can."

Once again, however, Shirley had made an unpopular political decision. When she tried to forge a coalition of representatives to vote for repeal of abortion laws regard less of their party loyalties, she failed. She was forced to put aside the bill she had carefully drafted for the repeal of abortion laws until a time when pressure from the people might make such a bill more acceptable in Congress.

Meanwhile, back home, Shirley had once more been displaying her political independence. Her first year in Congress was also a mayoral election year in New York City. The two major candidates were Mario Procaccino, a Democrat and city comptroller under the previous administration, and John V. Lindsay, the incumbent mayor. Lindsay had won election to office in 1965 on the Republican ticket, but during his first term many in his party had become dissatisfied with him. In 1969 he had failed to win the renomination of his own party and had been forced to run on the Liberal ticket.

John V. Lindsay, ca. 1969-77.
Photograph by Bernard Gotfryd.
Courtesy of the Library of Congress.

As a congresswoman, Shirley was expected to support publicly one of the mayoral candidates, and as a Democrat, she was expected to endorse Procaccino. But in all conscience Shirley could not support the Democrat. While she felt Lindsay had made mistakes during his first term as mayor, she considered him much more forward-looking and much more in tune with the times than Procaccino. In her heart she wanted to support Lindsay.

When she discussed her feelings with Conrad, Mac, and other close advisers, this time it was they who warned her against acting on her feelings. The Democratic Party was so powerful in the city that they were afraid of the consequences if Shirley broke with the party. With even those closest to her advising her against it, the decision to support Lindsay was one of the hardest Shirley ever had to make. Yet her conviction to vote her conscience and not to bow to political expediency was too strong. She called Lindsay and announced her support.

Shirley spent as much time as she could campaigning for Lindsay, and her support proved of immense value to him.

Although Shirley never claimed credit for Lindsay's victory in November, she knew very well that her endorsement, coming when it did, had helped him a great deal. Later she would ask that he return the favor.

As expected, the New York Democratic leaders were furious with Shirley. Procaccino and the Westchester County Democratic Committee chairman demanded that she be unseated as a national committeewoman. Many New York Black leaders informed her that there was little hope for her political future, but Shirley refused to let these reactions bother her.

"I told them that no one has a right to call himself a leader unless he dares to lead. That means standing up to be counted on the side of his people, even at the risk of his political security. It means giving clear direction, so the people do not have to guess where you stand." Once again Shirley seems to have made a dangerous decision and emerged unscathed. She was not unseated as a national committeewoman, and in 1970, when she ran for reelection to Congress, she received 82 percent of the vote. She may not have sponsored any major legislation, but she had proved an independent spokeswoman for many people both in and outside her district in Brooklyn, people who desperately needed someone to speak for them.

Shirley took the oath of office for the second time in 1971. She knew her way around now and she knew her fellow members of Congress much better than she had two years before. She also had learned that if she was to get anywhere on Capitol Hill she would have to bend a little to congressional custom. Having once gone through the experience of fighting for a committee spot that even remotely concerned her, she did not want to do it again. Education and Labor was her first choice; it was the committee on which she felt most qualified to serve and on which she felt she could do the most good, and so this time she took a practical approach. In the election of a new majority leader, she voted for Southerner Hale Boggs. In the election to fill a spot on the Rules Committee, she voted for another Southerner, Joe D. Waggoner, Jr. Both were influential senior members of Congress. As a result, when the question of her own committee assignment came up, she received a spot on the Education and Labor Committee. During the early 1960s this committee, under the chairmanship of Adam Clayton Powell, had reported out some of the most far-reaching and forward-looking legislation ever to come out of the House of Representatives.

"I have to be practical," she told Conrad. "Sometimes you have to give a little in order to get a lot. Education and Labor was where I wanted to be all the time, but I wouldn't have gotten on that committee for years if I hadn't compromised a little."

She found too that her publicly announced decision to vote No on every defense appropriation bill until the United States got out of Vietnam had to be modified later. Although she remained firmly against U.S. involvement in the war, she found that some defense-spending bills provided money for operations that were not involved in the war at all. She also found that if she were willing to compromise on such bills (voting Aye instead of No), there were other congressmen willing to vote Aye instead of No on some of the bills she favored.

In short, Shirley found that on Capitol Hill it was necessary to compromise—a little. But she did not become a sellout. Her continued popularity as a speaker on college campuses and among women's groups attested to that. She had simply come of age as a congresswoman.

Still, she hadn't much seniority. Second-term members of Congress fared little better than first-term members in introducing bills. By this time, however, she had a clear idea of the role she wanted to play as a congresswoman, and it did not include being a lawmaker.

"The housing laws, the equal employment opportunity laws, many more laws that are already on the books are not being used," she said. "We don't need any more legislation for a while. What we need is a Congress—and an administration—that will permit the ones we have to work."

Shirley knew that neither that type of Congress nor that type of administration was in power just then. Still, she was sure that as a congresswoman there was much she could do individually to make existing laws work for the people she represented.

Many of these laws provided for money grants to local organizations to be used to better the communities they served. In her position, Shirley was able to find out about the provisions of these laws and to help the people in her district take advantage of them. She managed to get more than $1 million for the Charles Drew Neighborhood Health Center, $150,000 for the Brooklyn Local Economic Development Center, and nearly half a million dollars for the Consumer Action Program in Bedford-Stuyvesant. In addition she secured money to help start the Cheetah Charter Bus Service Company, owned and run by Blacks, and to help the Afro-American Teachers Association continue its scholarship program for minority students. She also secured grants for Washington, D.C., organizations working in that city's minority neighborhoods.

Many of the existing laws also contained antidiscrimination clauses. Shirley, and the staffs of her offices in Washington, D.C., and Brooklyn used these clauses to help countless individuals secure housing, jobs, daycare services, and welfare. While she was becoming an increasingly well-known personality nationally, she did not neglect the local people whom she served and who continued to provide her chief power base.

All in all then, Shirley proved a rather unorthodox congress-woman. She was Black, she was a woman, and she was very independent. Though she had made a few compromises in order to get what she wanted, she had not made them to benefit herself but to help the people whom she represented. Otherwise she would never have come out in favor of abortion-law repeal or have supported John Lindsay for a second term. In addition she was unorthodox in that she was a lawmaker who was not really interested in making laws. She considered herself more of a spokeswoman for those who were not well represented in Congress and a "law fulfiller." She felt America already had all the laws it needed.

"What it lacks," she said, "is the heart, the humanity, and the Christian love that it would take. It is perhaps unrealistic to hope that I can help give this nation any of those things, but that is what I believe I have to try to do."

And in her characteristic manner, Shirley chose a rather unorthodox way to try.

7.
SHIRLEY CHISHOLM FOR PRESIDENT

Shirley had been nurturing in the back of her mind the possibility of running for president long before the campaigns for the 1972 presidential election began. College students had first given her the idea.

"I can't remember exactly when or where it happened," she now says, "but it was at a southern school. A young white student asked me why I didn't run for president, and I gave him the answer I had been giving for three years, laughing as I said it: 'You don't know what you're asking me to do. You must understand, whatever my ability to handle the job, and regardless of your belief in me, I am Black and I am a woman.' The young man would not accept my answer. 'Well, when are we going to break this tradition?' he demanded. 'We've had a lot of speakers here, and none of them has dealt with the issues the way you have. We need somebody who will do that.'

"His question stayed with me for some reason. When were we going to break this tradition? Looking back, I can see the germ of the decision began there."

Shirley was not the only Black politician thinking along these lines in 1970 and 1971. Black political activity had increased greatly since 1968. Each election year brought more Black officeholders on state and local levels, more Black mayors of major cities, more Blackcongressmen. As a result of the protests at the 1968 convention, new rules had been adopted within the

Democratic Party to assure to assure that Blacks would win at least three hundred seats at the 1972 presidential convention. Many Black political leaders felt that the Black vote could be a significant factor in the upcoming election—if it were organized and used properly.

How could they best influence the Democratic National Convention to be held in August 1972? There was little concern with the Republican Party. In the first place most Blacks were registered Democrats. In the second place there was little question that President Richard Nixon would be nominated to run for a second term. Although a few Black leaders argued that the Black vote was taken for granted by the Democratic Party and that it would shake up the party if Blacks were to show an interest in the Republicans, their arguments were unrealistic. President Nixon was making it quite clear during his first term that he had little concern for Black and other minority Americans. The important task was to show the Democrats that there was a Black voting bloc to be reckoned with.

It would be a complicated task because the whole system of choosing a presidential nominee was a complicated one. Democrats in each state chose delegates to the national convention by means of primary elections. On the primary ballots each delegate who ran was committed to a particular candidate, meaning that if he were elected to go to the national convention he would vote for that particular candidate. Practically anyone could be listed as a candidate. While the major candidates for the Democratic nomination—Senators Edmund S. Muskie of Maine, Hubert H. Humphrey of Minnesota, and George McGovern of South Dakota—would all be represented by slates of delegates in the primaries, each primary ballot would also have some delegates committed to minor candidates.

There could be a "favorite son" candidate, usually the governor of a state or some other popular officeholder who had no hope of getting the presidential nomination but who wished to take some delegates to the convention to bargain with. There could also be a "stalking horse" candidate, usually another popular officeholder who held views similar to those of a serious candidate; he would try to feel out the voters in the state about their reaction to those views, even though he himself did not intend to run.

Thus, a state that sent 145 delegates to the Democratic National Convention might come out of the primaries like this: 90 delegates committed to George McGovern, 25 delegates committed to Hubert Humphrey, 10 delegates committed to Edmund Muskie, 10 delegates committed to a favorite son candidate, and 10 delegates committed to a candidate who was really a stalking horse for New York Mayor John V. Lindsay (who was feeling out his chances of running for the Democratic nomination). Those last 20 delegates would be regarded as uncommitted when they reached the convention, and the major candidates would make efforts to win them over.

Julian Bond, 1966. Photograph by Warren K. Leffler. *Courtesy of the Library of Congress.*

In the summer of 1971 Black leaders were trying to decide the best way to keep Black votes uncommitted until the national convention. Representative Julian Bond of Georgia urged that each state or city with a good-sized Black population run a well-known Black favorite son candidate in the primaries. Each would bring a few delegates to the Democratic convention and meet there to decide how to combine them.

Some disagreed with Bond's idea. They urged that each major candidate be approached with a list of recommendations for bettering the lives of Black people and that Black support either be given or denied to the candidates on the basis of their response.

Still others felt that the time had come to run a Black presidential candidate. A Black candidate, if supported by all Blacks, would create a Black caucus with increased bargaining power at the convention. The candidate would not have any chance of being nominated, but he could bring unity among Blacks and carry considerable political clout.

Shirley agreed with this last position. She too had other reasons for favoring this strategy. A candidate with little chance of being nominated who addressed himself directly to the major issues of the campaign might help force the major candidates to address the issues more directly, instead of hedging as they usually did.

In July of 1971 Shirley began to drop hints that she might run in some primaries. She did this to see what kind of response she might get. She had talked with both Conrad and Mac Holder about the possibility of running, but they had not been much help. All they had been able to tell her was what she already knew. "It takes a lot of money, Shirley. Even the most well-funded campaigns go into debt. You are being urged to run by a lot of people who will not be able to contribute much money. They don't realize how much you will need. And there is something else you know that they don't know—your candidacy will stir up a lot of controversy. But if you decide to run, we'll back you completely."

The decision was hers. How was she going to decide? The initial feedback from the hints she had dropped was of little help. It was as mixed as her feelings were. College students urged her to run. Women's groups urged her to run; one group even had campaign buttons made that read, "Ms. Chiz for Pres." Black women urged her to run. Almost all politicians, Black and white, were against it.

In September Black politicians and civil rights leaders from across the country met in the Northlake section of Chicago to decide on the best course of action in the 1972 election. Though Shirley received an invitation to the meeting, she felt that it would be unwise for her to attend. There was as yet no unity among those at the meeting, and she foresaw that she would be the focus of much of the discussion if she were there. Instead, she sent her chief political aide, Thaddeus Garrett.

Reports from Garrett confirmed Shirley's intuitions. The general opinion at the meeting was that she would not be recognized as a candidate for Blacks but for women. She stressed "women's issues" too much for the tastes of most of the Black politicians and civil rights leaders who attended the meeting. Even if Shirley had confined herself to Black issues and had not addressed women's issues, she would not have been endorsed at the meeting. One participant at the meeting expressed the general sentiment when he told a *Washington Post* reporter, "In this first serious effort of Blacks for high political office, it would be better if it were a man." Shirley would encounter that kind of feeling again and again, but her reaction was, "The Black man must step forward but that doesn't mean that Black women have to step back." She was surprised, however, that one of the Black elected officials had actually expressed publicly his antifemale prejudices. It was another example of how she encountered more discrimination as a woman than as a Black in politics.

Obviously those at the meeting were not taking her seriously. The trouble was, it seemed to Shirley, that the men at the convention were not taking themselves seriously. Or perhaps it was that, individually, they were taking themselves too seriously—refusing to compromise and come together on one plan of action. "This is very distressing to me," she told reporters who asked her to comment on the efforts of the Black male politicians. "As of this moment, the Black elected officials have not really come up with their strategy. Meanwhile, people are moving, and the essence is time. This is politics…. In good conscience, I can't hold back."

Some of Shirley's critics, and some disinterested observers as well, suggested that she really made no effort or had any desire to join with the male Black elected officials to discuss strategy. Instead, they argued, she herself had determined at an early stage to enter the presidential race and thus felt that there was nothing to discuss. Her statement that she had decided to enter the campaign only after becoming disillusioned with the progress of the meetings among Black politicians was nonsense, they said. Whatever the moment of Shirley's decision—before or after the meetings—it was clear to those who knew her well that Congresswoman Shirley Chisholm would soon be presidential candidate Shirley Chisholm.

Yet many people refused to believe she was a serious contender. When Shirley had first started to drop hints about running for the Democratic nomination, some political observers had concluded that she was acting as a stalking horse for New York's Mayor John

V. Lindsay. She and Lindsay had been quite close since she endorsed him for a second term as mayor in 1969, and they shared similar views on many issues. If Lindsay were to run, he would need the Black vote, and Shirley, as his stalking horse, could help him get it. Others thought she was a stalking horse for Humphrey or for McGovern. The fact that she did not attend the meeting at Northlake seemed to support the idea that she was indeed a stalking horse for some white candidate.

"People either see me as the Blacks' candidate or the women's candidate, or not a candidate at all, merely a 'stalking horse,'" Shirley complained to Conrad and Mac. "What they do not realize is that I could be the candidate for everyone the major candidates do not bother with. I've got potential support from all the minorities: Black, brown, and red, women, students, and even some older white voters who are tired of the runaround the usual major party candidates give them."

"No one is going to see you as the people's candidate until you say you are, Shirley," the two men closest to her advised. "No one is going to take you seriously until you announce your candidacy."

"But I haven't enough money to be a candidate," Shirley protested. "I'll wait until January. If enough money has come in by then, I'll make my announcement and enter the March Florida primary."

In December 1971 John Lindsay invited Shirley to Gracie Mansion, the official home for New York mayors. The mayor asked her directly if she planned to enter the Florida primary. Shirley said she did. She knew Lindsay was worried about what her presence would do to his chances. He was counting on a good showing in the Florida primary to prove that he was a real contender in the race for the nomination. Shirley would cut into the votes he was hoping to get. Lindsay could see, however, that Shirley had made up her mind. Her ability to make up her own mind had helped him two years before. He could not question it now. The two never discussed the subject again.

By the middle of January 1972, campaign money was continuing to come in, but it was still only a trickle. "You can't expect people to contribute very much to a campaign that doesn't even exist," Conrad and Mac reminded her. Shirley had to admit they were right. She decided to make a campaign trip to Florida to feel out the voters on her chances in the March primary.

Once there Shirley found little enthusiasm for her candidacy among Black elected officials. Some were trying to follow Julian Bond's plan and be Black favorite son candidates. Others felt she was on an "ego trip" and weakening the chances for a Black coalition in Florida. But among students, women's groups, and various other groups, Black and white, Shirley found enthusiastic support. They gave her cause for hope. She hired a campaign manager from a public relations firm, set up a campaign office in Washington, D.C., to maintain contact with the various campaign headquarters being set up by her supporters in Florida, and did all the other things a serious candidate does to get an organization going. There was no doubt in her mind now that she would run.

She knew hers was not a sensible decision. She would be lucky to get even a few delegates in Florida or in the other states where delegates were split among the candidates according to the percentage of the votes they received. In states such as Massachusetts and California the candidate who received the most votes won all the delegates. She didn't have a chance in such states.

"But all that seemed to me only another facet of the system I was out to shake up," Shirley explains. "And we weren't going to shake it up unless we got out and ran. The strategy was to plunge in and see what happened. Either the support came together or it didn't, but nothing would happen unless we made a try."

Shirley Chisholm, ca. 1972. *Photograph by Bernard Gotfryd. Courtesy of the Library of Congress.*

On January 25, 1972, Shirley called a press conference at Brooklyn's largest Baptist church. The church was packed with reporters and well-wishers as she made her formal announcement:

> "I stand before you today as a candidate for the Democratic nomination for the presidency of the United States. I am not the candidate of Black America, although I am Black and proud. I am not the candidate of the women's movement of this country, although I am a woman, and I am equally proud of that. I am not the candidate of any political bosses or special interests.... I am the candidate of the people."

She spoke of the problems that troubled the nation: the Vietnam War, economic recession, the destruction of the environment, the loss of a feeling of community, the suspicions of corruption in politics, the sense of the powerlessness of the individual. She spoke of the vast potential of the country and its people and how, in the past, this potential had been neglected by old-line politicians who were more interested in political expediency than in what was right. She continued:

> "We must turn away from the prosaic, the privileged, and the old-line, tired politicians to open our society to the energies and abilities of countless groups of Americans— women, Blacks, browns, Indians, Orientals, and youth—so that they can develop their own full potential and thereby participate equally and enthusiastically in building a strong and just society, rich in its diversity and noble in its quality of life."

She had done it. She had committed herself to being the first Black woman ever to run for the presidential nomination of a major party. She was in fact only the second woman ever to run. (In 1964 Senator Margaret Chase Smith of Maine had entered two primaries for the Republican presidential nomination.) Shirley had committed herself to speaking out on behalf of neglected Americans. She had also committed herself to six months of exhausting travel and speech-making, of trying to be a candidate and a congresswoman at the same time, of being the brunt of racism and sexism, of disastrous factionalism among her supporters, and of debts piling up one on top of another.

Her campaign in Florida set the tone for her campaign as a whole. Although her announcement of formal candidacy started to bring in more money, as Conrad and Mac had predicted, it still was not enough to wage a major campaign. Altogether Shirley made three trips to Florida and spent practically all the money she had on them. Her campaign organization in the state was really a series of organizations, each with different ideas about where Shirley should go and what she should say. In a sense the situation could not be otherwise. All her workers were volunteers who received no money from her. Because she refused to choose leaders from among them, they struggled against one another for power.

Women's groups complained that Blacks were trying to take over. Blacks complained that women were trying to take over. Women portrayed Shirley as a women's candidate; Blacks campaigned for her as a Black candidate. One woman in Tampa, who wanted a juvenile center for the city, told reporters covering one of Shirley's visits, "Now look, we're not going to promote this political stuff. She's here to publicize juvenile problems."

Often public appearances had to be canceled and rescheduled several times because of Shirley's congressional commitments. Now that she was on the committee of her choice, the House

Shirley Chisholm's presidential campaign poster reading, "Bring U.S. together. Vote Chisholm 1972, unbought and unbossed." N.G. Slater Corporation. *Courtesy of the Library of Congress.*

Education and Labor Committee, Shirley wanted to be a responsible member. If a crucial vote was coming up, she had to be there despite the consequences to her campaign.

Her hired campaign manager, Gerald Robinson, quit in frustration. Shirley recalls, "Gerry wrote me a letter pointing out the problems we were having because I was trying to function as a campaign manager as well as a candidate, while at the same time trying to hold up my end as a member of Congress."

Shirley worried about the lack of organization in her campaign, but without a paid staff there was little she could do to better the situation. All she could hope to do was win votes by the sheer strength of her personality and her ideas—and do this while spending only about ten days in Florida.

What she had to do was take a firm stand on the issues in the campaign, and the issue that seemed to concern Florida voters most was busing to correct racial imbalance in the schools. It was the main theme of the Florida campaign of George Wallace, who was expected to win the primary. Shirley was asked her position on that issue everywhere she went.

"Busing," she would always answer, "is an artificial way of solving the segregation problem. Open housing is the real answer. But as long as the problem exists, an artificial solution is better than no solution at all. Where were you," she asked the whites, "when for years Black children were being bused out of their neighborhoods and carried miles on old rattletrap buses, down back roads to a dirty school with a tarpaper roof and no toilets? If you believed in neighborhood schools, where were you then? I'm not going to shed any crocodile tears for you now that you've discovered the busing problem."

It was not the sort of thing one would expect a candidate for the presidency to say in the South. Humphrey, Muskie, and McGovern all hemmed and hawed on the issue when they were campaigning in the South. Many people, whether they agreed with Shirley or not, respected her for her honesty, and George Wallace himself began to note respectfully that Shirley Chisholm was the only other candidate besides himself who said the same things in the South as in the North.

When the primary votes were in, Shirley had received about 4 percent of the vote. She had hoped for 5 or 6 percent, but even 4 percent made her resolve to continue her campaign. John Lindsay, meanwhile, had received slightly over 6 percent of the vote, and his try for the Democratic nomination was over. His supporters charged that Shirley had hurt him, that if she had not run, he would have received the needed 10 percent. Shirley scoffed at these charges. After all, if Lindsay had not run, perhaps she would have received 10 percent of the vote.

Having gotten her feet wet in the Florida primary, Shirley had to decide which other primaries to enter. Money was a major factor; she did not have much and had to concentrate on running in those states where she was pretty sure of getting some delegates. Time was another factor—she could not take too much time away from her congressional duties.

Washington, D.C.'s primary would have been perfect for her to enter. Because she had to be there anyway, travel expenses would be minimal and she could attend congressional sessions and campaign practically at the same time. Then, too, she was very popular in Washington, D.C., and could expect many votes. But Walter Fauntroy asked her not to enter that primary. He planned to enter as a favorite son and promised to release his delegates to her on the second ballot at the convention. "I was skeptical about his promise," Shirley remembers, "but he reminded me that he was a minister, so I went along."

In March, April, and May, Shirley campaigned in New Jersey, Massachusetts, California, Michigan, and North Carolina, but she was unable to devote enough time to any of those states because of her congressional duties. Congresswoman Chisholm's attendance record in Congress during her first two terms should be a lesson to those in Congress who continue blindly to support the seniority system in giving committee assignments instead of considering the qualifications and desires of individual representatives. During her first term, when she served on the Veterans Committee, Shirley's attendance record was only 55 percent. In the first session of her second term, when she was finally given a spot on the Education and Labor Committee, her attendance was 72 percent. In the second session of her second term, despite the fact that she was campaigning for the presidential nomination, her attendance was still better than 55 percent, which was above the average attendance in the House of Representatives.

In each state her campaign consisted of a day here and a weekend there. In each state she encountered many eager volunteers who were willing to set up campaign headquarters and expected no money from Shirley's Washington campaign base. Yet in almost every state her supporters were riddled by factionalism, primarily between the women and the young Black men. Shirley kept hoping they would somehow get together, forget their petty concerns, and join together to work for a common goal, but she was being unrealistic in her hope.

"I had to spend time with both groups," Shirley recalls, "trying to smooth things out, trying to convince them that there was more to the campaign than their concerns.... The women were politically naïve; they were enthusiastic, but they did not understand the first thing about politics. Even more than Blacks, I think, they showed the effects of their past exclusion from the political process, and unlike Blacks, they found it hard to believe that they had a great deal to learn."

The only times the gap between feminists and Blacks was bridged was when Black or brown women active in the women's movement were on hand. "Having long been active in the civil rights movement and other minority causes, they were used to taking up seemingly impossible challenges," Shirley says. "Their whole experience had taught them that they might not win the ultimate objective, but they would make some gains and in the process increase the chance that success would come, someday."

Meanwhile Shirley traveled from state to state continuing to say what she felt rather than what her listeners wanted to hear. In Michigan, a state divided over court-ordered busing and often called "Wallace country—north," she repeated the opinion on busing that she had expressed in Florida. She also addressed herself to two other unpopular subjects in Michigan, welfare and tax reform:

> "We Americans need to lift the burdens of unfairness and discrimination from the shoulders of so many of our fellow countrymen, of both sexes, all ages, and all races. This is why I call for tax reform, to ensure that each man pays his fair share based on his income; that is why I call for welfare reform and a national system of daycare centers."

In Boston's Roxbury section, a predominantly Black neighborhood, the audience that assembled to hear Shirley in the Charles Street African Methodist Episcopal Church was shocked to see several young men dressed in women's clothing make their conspicuous entrance. "Hiya, Shirley! Right on, gal!" cried one strikingly dressed young man.

They were there because she had declared that homosexuals should enjoy the same rights and privileges as heterosexuals. Shirley did not snub them because the rest of her audience was shocked. On the contrary she greeted them cordially and thanked them for their support.

Despite all the strong stands she took on major issues, Shirley was criticized for not having a platform. A platform is a list of issues and the stands taken on them by a candidate. At the Democratic convention in August an official Democratic platform would be decided and voted upon. Looking back on the campaign, it would seem that Shirley had just as much of a platform as any of the other candidates and, indeed, that her platform remained more consistent from state to state and from region to region than did those of the other candidates. However, Shirley did campaign more on the basis of her own qualifications and personality than did the others. Though one woman reporter's statement that "Shirley Chisholm's platform is Shirley Chisholm" was extreme, it contained some truth.

"They talk about my qualifications," she told a group of high school students in Miami. "'Shirley,' they say, 'what qualifications do you have to presume to be President of the United States?' Well, I have a near-genius IQ, if that means anything. I'm ten credits away from a Ph.D., if that means anything. I'm the only candidate who speaks Spanish fluently… What else do you want?"

"I had to campaign on the issue of myself," Shirley says. "That's partly what my fight was all about. The others could point to years of experience in the Senate or in the House or as governor of some state. What could I point to but years of working my way up through grassroots politics, fighting past barriers every step of the way, partly because I was Black but mostly because I was a woman. I made it within the system in spite of the system, and that was one of the major thrusts of my campaign. It was all those men who'd had years of experience in law and in Congress and as governors who'd gotten us into the mess we're in in the first place. The people I was trying to reach were tired of hearing about all their meaningless qualifications and platforms that crumbled into sawdust once they got elected."

Like a tiny dynamo, Shirley did her best to shake up the system, and as primary after primary took place, the results showed that while she didn't cause any earthquakes, she was responsible for a sizable tremor here and there.

In the Wisconsin primary Shirley received 9,100 votes. Although it was less than 1 percent of the vote, it was more than she had expected. In the Massachusetts primary, which she entered on the spur of the moment, she got 23 percent of the vote, and in North Carolina she came in third, with 9 percent of the vote. However, the Massachusetts primary was a winner-take-all contest, and in North Carolina, 15 percent of the vote was necessary before a candidate could win any delegates. Minnesota primary laws provided for delegates to be apportioned to all candidates based on percentage of vote and in this, Hubert Humphrey's home state, Shirley picked up eight delegates.

Although Shirley was pleased with her showing in some of the primaries, she was disappointed overall. Throughout the campaign she continually had to deal with questions about the seriousness of her bid for the presidency.

"You don't really expect to win, do you?" people asked. "Which white male candidate do you think will win?"

Such questions irked Shirley. No, she did not expect to win. That was not the point. The point of her campaign was to give the neglected groups in American society a real choice. Through their votes for her they could show the major candidates that they were a force to be reckoned with. But many who expressed support for her on the campaign trail did not translate that support into votes. If they had, her vote totals would have been higher in every state primary that she entered.

Looking back on her poor showing in the Michigan primary, she says, "Perhaps it was that people who sympathized with me still considered that they would be wasting their votes on me; politics in this country is a game that most people feel should be played to win, and it was hard for me to persuade them to use their votes to 'shake up the system within the system,' as I kept urging."

Just before the Michigan primary, the news came that George Wallace had been shot. Shirley's immediate reaction was a combination of shock, disgust, and fear. She was shocked and disgusted at America's seeming penchant for killing its most well-known public figures. The Kennedys, Martin Luther King, Malcolm X, now George Wallace—when would it ever stop, she wondered. She was afraid because she did not know whether or not Wallace had been killed and whether or not his assailant was Black. If a Black had shot Wallace, Shirley was ready to give up the campaign immediately. There would surely be retaliation, and she would be a likely target.

Shirley was later relieved to hear that Wallace was alive and that a white man had shot him, but she was still deeply disturbed. Like any public figure she had received her share of hate mail and threatening phone calls, but the Wallace shooting had brought home the real danger to which she exposed herself every time she left the sanctuary of her home.

It was partly because of this feeling and partly because of a genuine feeling of sympathy for Wallace that she visited him at Holy Cross Hospital in Maryland, where he was recuperating. "You and I don't agree," she told Wallace at one point during her twenty-minute visit, "but you've been shot, and I might be shot, and we are both the children of American democracy, so I wanted to come and see you."

When Shirley emerged from the hospital, the press was waiting en masse to question her, and across the country people speculated on the motives behind her visit. "There were Black politicians who insinuated that some kind of deal was being cooked up!" Shirley recalls. "One Black man from Texas, a delegate pledged to me, was so angry that he threatened to withdraw his support. What hurdles we Americans must still have to clear as we grope our way toward a civilized society, when such a simple gesture is deemed newsworthy and a sign of political intrigue!"

By this time Shirley was campaigning for the California primary, and in California she received a sign that she was considered somewhat important. Having received 5 percent of the vote in the national polls, she suddenly found herself assigned a detachment of Secret Servicemen. "Well, Conrad, we've really made it!" she laughingly announced to her husband.

Conrad, who had been traveling with Shirley as often as possible, could not have been happier. First, he was glad that Shirley finally had the protection he felt she needed. Second, as an investigator himself, he was eager to talk with the agents, who took an immediate liking to him.

The agents would be with them right through the Miami convention whether the Chisholms were in San Francisco or in Brooklyn. In Brooklyn Conrad and Shirley fixed up a downstairs room for them, complete with card tables and a television set. Only much later did they learn that Secret Service agents were not used to such hospitality and that the "Chisholm detail" became the most coveted in the campaign. After the convention the chief of the detachment presented Shirley with a scrapbook containing each day's itinerary during the weeks the Secret Service had been with her and a picture of every agent who had been assigned to her. It is still one of her most prized possessions.

Shirley came in third in the June California primary with 157,435 votes. Although she placed far behind McGovern with 1,550,000 votes and Humphrey with 1,375,000 votes, her total still would have entitled her to twelve delegates. But California was one of the states with a winner-take-all primary, and thus all its delegates would be pledged to George McGovern. Shirley, a bit discouraged and tired after having campaigned so hard with no tangible result, thought for the hundredth time that if she ever rose to a position of power in the national Democratic Party, the winner-take-all primary would be one of her first targets.

With the Democratic National Convention a month away, Shirley had 28 delegates. She would hardly be in a position of strength going into the convention, but she had been campaigning for six months and had entered eleven primaries, so she was not going to give up now. She rested awhile, made a few more public appearances, and hoped that the Black male politicians who had fought her or ignored her during the campaign would change their minds. An event occurred late in June, however, that caused this hope to become even slimmer than it already was.

When Shirley had first announced her candidacy, Walter Fauntroy, the nonvoting delegate to Congress from the District of Columbia had pleaded with her not to enter the Washington, D.C., primary, in which he planned to run as a favorite son candidate. He had promised, however, to release his delegates to her at the convention. On June 26, to Shirley's dismay, Fauntroy and two other prominent Black politicians, Louis Stokes of Ohio and William Clay of Missouri, announced in a press conference that they controlled, among them, 96 delegates, whom they were delivering to McGovern in return for his endorsement (with reservations) of the program of a recently held Gary, Indiana, National Black Political Convention. "When a preacher gets involved in politics," Shirley remarked to Conrad, "he becomes just another politician." That seemed the end of her hopes for any delegates from Washington, D.C.

The 1972 Democratic National Convention was very different from the 1968 convention, at least on the surface. In 1968

Shirley Chisholm at the Democratic National Convention in Miami Beach, FL, 1972. *Photograph by Thomas J. O'Halloran. Courtesy of the Library of Congress.*

television viewers had watched in horror as Chicago police battled young people, minorities, and women as they protested their exclusion from the political process; in 1972, as television cameras panned over the delegates in the Miami convention hall, the protesters of four years before now appeared to be inside. Delegations were more representative and included women, young people, and minorities. Those delegations that were not representative were challenged for their seats by alternative delegations that were. Yet machine politics still prevailed, and the desire to get behind a winner was as strong among the new delegates as among the old. The apparent winner, of course, was George McGovern. Advocates of women's liberation felt that if McGovern were elected president he would reward their support by championing measures favorable to women. Blacks hoped to be rewarded by measures favorable to Blacks. And so on. But since they were acting and dealing separately, none of these groups was in a position to demand the rewards they sought. Had all these groups been willing or able to unite and act in a single-minded manner, they would have been in a position to demand. This had been the major theme of Shirley's campaign, but too few had listened. Thus, though the many new young and female and Black and brown, and red faces on the convention floor appeared to signify change, in most ways they did not affect the workings of the convention any more than if they had been the usual white male faces.

Presidential nominating conventions last several days. The first few days are taken up by legal questions, such as delegation challenges and rules challenges. During this time the candidates and their supporters work hard in last-ditch efforts to attract more delegates to their side. Also at this time many candidates who feel they have no chance of winning drop out of the race and release their delegates, who are then eagerly sought by the other candidates. When all the challenges and questions on rules have been decided, the convention hears nominating speeches for candidates still in the race and a candidate is chosen. After that, a vice-presidential candidate is decided upon as well as the official party platform for the presidential campaign.

During the first few days of the convention Shirley's supporters visited delegation after delegation trying to find additional delegates for her. They concentrated on the 452 Black delegates, for at this point most of the women delegates not already committed to Shirley were firmly behind McGovern. Shirley's workers had some success: they picked up 23 delegates from Ohio, 21 from Louisiana, 12 from Mississippi, 9 from Pennsylvania, and 2 from Florida. One reason for this success was that many Black delegates who came to the convention committed to McGovern were having second thoughts. They were beginning to feel that perhaps they had been sold out.

The unrest had begun after the Fauntroy press conference of June 26. In the days that followed Fauntroy's announcement it was revealed that many of the 96 delegates he, Stokes, and Clay claimed to control had never been consulted on the matter. Other Blacks questioned the depth of McGovern's commitment. McGovern had announced back in the middle of 1971 that he could endorse the program proposed by the congressional Black caucus. Many asked just what, in definite terms, was he prepared to do for Blacks.

By the opening of the convention more Blacks were rethinking their positions, and Shirley saw a chance to forge at least a Black coalition.

Shirley Chisholm at the Democratic National Convention in Miami Beach, FL, 1972. *Photograph by Warren K. Leffler. Courtesy of the Library of Congress.*

She pleaded with the Black delegates, who were meeting in caucus, to think seriously about their votes:

> "Brothers and sisters! Think! You didn't come here to be delivered! Don't play yourselves cheap! You paid your own way here, and you worked hard to do it. A Black boss is as bad as a white boss, and some Black leaders are willing to advance their own political fortunes at the expense of the masses. Please! Think of yourselves! ... Go with me on the first ballot! And if you can't go with me, go uncommitted! Black people all over this country are watching what we do here!"

Shirley's experiences in politics had taught her that miracles could happen, or if not miracles exactly, then certainly the unexpected. Yet when she looked around the room after making her plea, she was quite certain that there would be no miracle this time. As things turned out, the Black caucus finally rejected McGovern and voted to endorse Shirley, but the move came just hours before the nominations—about six months too late.

Shirley was officially nominated on Wednesday night, July 12, by Percy Sutton, Black president of the Borough of Manhattan in New York City. Her nomination was seconded by Charles Evers, Black mayor of Fayette, Mississippi, who begged the Black delegates to vote for her on the first ballot "so the Black poor and other people who have been left out for so long will not be in someone's pocket on the first ballot."

When the nominations were over, voting on the first ballot began. In order to win the party's nomination, a candidate must get a majority of the delegates' votes. Sometimes a contest is so close that ballot after ballot must be taken. Each state delegation is polled in alphabetical order until eventually enough delegates change their votes to give one of the candidates a majority. At the Democratic convention of 1972, 1,415 delegates constituted a majority, and George McGovern had received that many votes even be for all the state delegations were polled. At that point Shirley had 151.25 votes. She would have received more votes from the remaining states, but it is customary, once a candidate has a majority, for the remaining delegates to switch to that candidate. Thus George McGovern would be the Democratic candidate in the 1972 presidential election, and Shirley's long campaign was over.

The rest of the convention was anticlimactic. There was a brief attempt on the part of some of those groups who felt they had been sold out to put a woman or a Black on the Democratic ticket as Vice-President. Shirley was mentioned, but she was not interested in being the tool of a token opposition. A white male was chosen as the vice-presidential candidate. The women who had pushed for a female candidate had not really expected to be successful. However they were angry and bitter over another failure. They had expected McGovern to support an abortion plank for the Democratic platform; instead his forces had defeated it. "Like the Blacks," Shirley later said, "the women had failed to get it together at Miami; too many had made commitments to a candidate ahead of time, and their adherence to him made it impossible for them to work effectively for their cause."

On Thursday night, the last night of the convention, Shirley appeared with the other unsuccessful candidates behind McGovern and his vice-presidential choice, Thomas Eagleton, in a display of Democratic unity. It was a necessary public gesture that she did not believe in privately. For many months she had witnessed first-hand the factionalism in the party, and she seriously doubted the party's ability to come together and elect George McGovern president. She would support McGovern and do some campaigning for him, but for Shirley the presidential campaign was essentially over.

8.

THE FIGHT ISN'T OVER YET

After the Democratic convention in July 1972, Shirley took time to assess her campaign. There were many things that she would do differently if she ever again campaigned for the presidential nomination. First, she would plan ahead. She would declare her candidacy early in order to amass more contributions to finance her campaign and in order to give groups wishing to support her more time to get organized. She would make sure she had a campaign manager all through the campaign and would not try to act as her own manager. But there were some things she knew she could not change. She could not solve the disputes between women's groups and Black groups. She could not change the minds of those who liked what she said but did not have faith in the ability of a long-shot candidate to win. She could not single-handedly forge a coalition of all the groups whose support she sought. These things were up to the people; they had to get themselves together.

She had done what she could. Although her candidacy had not forged a solid coalition of those people working for social change, it had at least begun to form one. And there were many individuals across the country who would never be quite the same again. There were the women who had been inspired to work in a political campaign for the first time. There were the Blacks who had finally registered to vote, heartened by the chance to vote for a Black candidate. There were the students, professionals, and laborers, who had been impressed with a political figure who told the truth as she saw it no matter what the cost. There were the children, changed by the sight of a

Black woman saying, "I want to be President." Many of these people wrote to Shirley to tell her of the effect she'd had on their lives, and she knew all the time and money and effort had not been wasted.

Shirley's life returned to its normal pace, although her pace would hardly be considered normal for most people. She accepted speaking invitations again and began work on a book about her campaign. Also, she plunged into legislative work in Congress.

Her first major effort was to save the Office of Economic Opportunity (OEO). The Nixon Administration wished to disband the office, which had served as a major distributor of funds to ghetto self-help programs, food programs, and other antipoverty programs for several years. The Administration and its supporters charged that many of the OEO-funded programs had failed, that funds had been misused, that too many mistakes had been made. Shirley agreed that there had been errors and inequities, but she felt that the successes of OEO far outweighed the failures. "Any kind of experimental social program in this country designed to move in the direction of giving people a new hold on life, giving them inspiration and stimulation, is bound to be fraught with some errors."

Shirley realized, however, that it would take more than arguments from herself and other legislators who supported OEO to convince those who were against it that they were wrong. She urged the House Education and Labor Committee to conduct hearings in cities across the country to learn from the people most closely involved what would happen if the OEO program was terminated and what changes might be made to make the program better. She was one of the committee members who conducted those hearings and who urged fellow representatives to attend them.

As she had hoped, many members changed their minds about OEO after traveling around with Shirley and listening to poor people tell about their lives and how they had been changed for the better by OEO. "After we returned from those trips, so often many of these congressmen said, "I didn't know things were that bad. I didn't understand before,'" Shirley recalls. "And some of them got to the point of confessing that they had never been in a room with so many Blacks…. It was a kind of confrontation with social ills such as they had never really emotionally experienced before."

Before the hearings were conducted, a majority of the representatives had been against the OEO. After the hearings the House voted to continue the OEO and its programs. "I was very proud to have had a role in helping to change attitudes in Congress and helping to save the OEO program," Shirley commented.

Since that time, the Office of Economic Opportunity has been rendered virtually ineffective. Under the Nixon Administration, many of its programs were cut back or terminated altogether and overall funding was reduced drastically. These steps were taken unilaterally by the Administration, without consulting the Congress, and the matter is a source of great frustration and anger to Shirley Chisholm. At that time, however, Shirley could not foresee the steps that would be taken against OEO, and, encouraged by her seeming success in maintaining its vitality, she took up another cause that was dear to her heart—the inclusion of domestic workers among those groups covered by the minimum-wage law.

A bill to include domestic workers under minimum wage coverage had been introduced in 1972 and had been voted down. Shirley determined that in 1973 it would not be voted down. In April she began a campaign to assure domestic workers of the pay they were due. First she circulated a petition in favor of the legislation among the fifteen members of the women's caucus, which was comprised of all the women in the House of Representatives. All but two signed it. Then she began putting favorable remarks about the bill into the Congressional Record. She talked to fellow members of Congress while her staff people held meetings with women's groups, labor groups, and others who were interested in the bill.

Women and labor were the two major groups who had an interest in the bill, and it was no simple job to get them to unite behind it. Labor was against the proposed constitutional amendment granting equal rights to women, and much bitterness between the groups was the result. But Shirley and her staff managed to bring them together. It was, many said later, Shirley's finest performance as a congresswoman. She organized a congressional office to serve as a command post in the fight for the bill. Under her supervision her aides talked with women's groups and labor groups and secured their support. She and her aides lined up a majority of representatives behind the bill. The result of all this hard work was a House vote of 287 to 130 on June 6 to increase the minimum wage for nearly 35 million workers from $1.60 to $2.20 an hour within a year and to extend the wage coverage to domestic workers for the first time. One of the most important factors, it seemed to many observers, was that she did all this behind the scenes, almost anonymously. Shirley Chisholm rarely acted anonymously!

In newspaper and magazine articles reporters wrote that she was changing from a celebrity to a legislator. When asked to comment, Shirley explained that the matter was not that simple, either for her or for the members of the congressional Black caucus. She reminded her audiences that the majority of Black congressmen did not have the seniority necessary to push proposed legislation out of committee and onto the floor for action.

"That's what's so terrible about this system," she said, "that the committee chairmen have such control. Sometimes you hear people say, 'Adam Clayton Powell did so much, and you other Black congressmen aren't moving like Adam.'

"But people forget to also mention that Adam Powell was chairman of one of the most powerful committees in the House of Representatives, the Committee of Education and Labor, and as such he could sway legislation to do what he had to do. If Shirley Chisholm ever becomes chairman of a committee, and doesn't try to do what Adam did, then slap me up against the wall!"

In pointing out how difficult it was for Black members of Congress to be effective legislators, Shirley was not excusing herself and her fellow Blacks in the caucus. She was merely trying to explain their situation.

"What we tried to do originally, when there were only the first thirteen of us, is be all things to all people. We were deluged and overwhelmed with legitimate grievances and concerns from our Black people all over the country. A few of us, who are more prone to be activistic,

Shirley Chisholm speaking at Black Caucus State of the Union event, 1973. *Photograph by Warren K. Leffler. Courtesy of the Library of Congress.*

started to go all over he place trying to put whatever weight and leverage we had behind being national congressmen.

"But we weren't doing our job legislatively back in Washington. It takes time to do homework legislatively. You've got to read. You've got to do research. You've got to prepare your debates. You've got to know how to strategize. You've got to talk with various groups."

By June 1973 Shirley had shown that she could indeed read and research and strategize and talk with various groups very effectively. She was working within the system, but at the same time she was trying to make it more responsive to the needs of the people whom she represented. She was hopeful about her ability to continue doing so. Then her hopes were dashed. The Minimum Wage Bill, after being passed by both the House and the Senate, was vetoed by President Nixon. Shirley had worked exhaustively for two months to get that bill passed in the House. Though she had not pushed it through single-handedly, she is credited by both women's and labor groups with being the most important factor in its passage. All her work had been for nothing. Just as she had seemed to make a truce with the system, the system, in the guise of the President's veto, had declared war once more.

Angry and discouraged, Shirley announced early in July 1973 that she intended to retire from politics "definitely by 1976, but I expect to get out before then. If I do run for Congress again in 1974, it will be my last campaign." She cited as her main reason "the ineffectiveness of Congress."

She wanted to establish a political institute in Washington that would be affiliated with four or five universities in the area. "I've visited over 100 campuses, and I've seen that young people want to learn some things about politics," she said. She wanted to travel, write, and lecture and live part of the year in the Virgin Islands. "I have no desire to be a career politician," she said.

Some supporters pleaded with her to reconsider her decision.

Others believed she did not really mean what she had said, that she was just frustrated. "Shirley is prone to highs and lows," they said. "She's down now, but she'll be back up fighting soon."

Several months passed. No word came that Shirley Chisholm had changed her mind. Then, a peculiar thing happened. The General Accounting Office (GAO) of the federal government released a report charging mishandling of funds in Shirley's campaign for the presidential nomination. Specifically, the report charged that $18,000 had been "possibly misused." This implied, of course, that Shirley and her husband had taken the money for themselves.

Another charge was that Shirley had failed to appoint a campaign manager. Still another was that her office had failed to return three corporate contributions in the amounts of $100, $200, and $386 after such contributions had been ruled illegal by the GAO.

President Nixon at the White House, 1973. *Courtesy of the National Archives Catalog.*

The report made newspaper headlines across the country, and the articles rarely failed to point out that Shirley and Conrad had built a fabulous home in the Virgin Islands or that she was considered one of the best-dressed women on Capitol Hill. Everywhere she went, Shirley was questioned repeatedly about the GAO charges.

She replied with her own charges. She stated that she believed the investigations were an attempt to "get her," and that she had been singled out by the Nixon Administration for "investigation and harassment" because of her independent political stance against most of the Administration's policies. She recalled what Adam Clayton Powell had told her when she had arrived in Washington in 1969 as a freshman congresswoman, and tears came to her eyes as she related the incident to reporters:

"Adam schooled me," she said. "He said, 'Shirley, if you are a simple, quiet Black woman and you don't speak out against the inequities, they'll leave you alone. But once you become outspoken, they will get you.'"

Well, Shirley decided, they were not going to get her! She was hurt by the slant taken in many of the articles about her, by the implications that because she and Conrad had a nice home in Brooklyn or a house in the Virgin Islands they must have used some of the campaign funds for their own personal purposes. The constant questions from reporters sometimes brought tears of frustration to her eyes. But Shirley was not the sort to let the GAO's charges or the publicity about these charges get her down for long. In fact, the charges proved to be just the thing to get her "back up fighting," as her supporters had hoped. "I will emerge from this investigation unscathed," she declared, "and prepared to run again for my seat."

In May 1974 the GAO announced that after conducting a thorough investigation into the finances of the Chisholm campaign, it had concluded that the charges of November were unfounded. No mishandling of funds had been proved. Shirley Chisholm had emerged victorious from yet another battle.

"I consider myself an historical person at this point," she says. She was the first Black congresswoman; she was the first Black woman to run for the presidential nomination. She is aware of being a "first" and feels a responsibility to women and to Blacks and to the other groups she represents. For these reasons it is unlikely that Shirley Chisholm will retire from politics in the near future.

There is, moreover, another reason Shirley is likely to hold on, to continue trying to work within the system to bring about change in the system. Although she professes not to take such things as fortune-telling and soothsaying seriously, she sometimes tells how her mother went to a soothsayer when Shirley was a child. The soothsayer told her mother that before Shirley was forty she would be the first of her race and sex in state office.

Shirley was forty years old when she was elected to the New York State Assembly.

The soothsayer said that before Shirley was fifty, she would be the first of her race and sex in national office.

Shirley was forty-four years old when she was elected to the U.S. House of Representatives.

The soothsayer said, finally, that before she was fifty-six, Shirley would occupy one of the two top positions in the nation.

In 1974 Shirley was forty-nine years old.

"It's all come true so far," says Shirley Chisholm.

APPENDIX

The Legislative Record of Shirley Chisholm

Each year, thousands of bills are introduced in every state legislature. Thousands more are introduced in the Congress of the United States. In order for a bill, whether state or federal, to become law, it must first be considered and recommended by the appropriate legislative committee. Then it must be passed by both houses (Assembly and Senate in a state legislature, House of Representatives and Senate in Congress) and signed by the highest official of the executive branch (the governor in the case of state legislation and the president in the case of national legislation). Needless to say, a bill can be stalled or "killed" at every step along the way, and of the thousands introduced each year only a comparative few are ever passed. Particularly in the U.S. Congress, the seniority of a member is very important to the success of a bill he or she has sponsored or co-sponsored.

New York State Assemblywoman Shirley Chisholm

1965 Session

Mrs. Chisholm introduced 113 bills; of these, the following were passed:

> Chapter 746, New York City Education Law, to provide that on review of trial hearings by the New York City Education Board, each member before voting shall review testimony and acquaint himself with the evidence in the case, instead of merely reading testimony after the report of the committee or trial examiner holding trial. (Principal sponsor.)

> Chapter 200, New York City Higher Education Law, to provide that when the service of a member of the instructional staff of an educational unit under the jurisdiction of the New York City higher education board is interrupted by absence on maternity leave duly granted by the board,

the period of creditable service immediately preceding such absence shall be counted in computing 3 full years of service for accrual of tenure rights. (Principal sponsor.)

Chapter 943, New York State Higher Education Law, to provide that expected duration of the experimental program for the purpose of identifying and encouraging potential abilities among pupils of culturally deprived groups (SEEK Program) shall not exceed 5 years from the date of the beginning of approved program in such district, instead of from July 1, 1962. (Principal sponsor.)

1966 Session

Mrs. Chisholm introduced or co-sponsored 36 bills; of these the following was passed:

Chapter 24, New York State Election Law, to provide that county committees of political parties may make rules that members of state committees shall possess duties, powers and functions of assembly district leaders or associate leaders, with such leaders automatically becoming members of the county committee. (Co-sponsor.)

1967 Session

Mrs. Chisholm introduced or co-sponsored 55 bills; of these the following were passed:

Chapter 586, New York City Administration Code, to authorize the parks commissioner to enter into an agreement with the Brooklyn Institute of Arts and Sciences for the maintenance and operation by the institute of a Brooklyn Children's Museum in Brower Park, Brooklyn Borough, with the agreement to be come effective only upon approval of the mayor. (Principal sponsor.)

Chapter 202, to amend Executive Law, Town Law, General City Law, Village Law, and to add to Membership Corporations Law, to make it unlawful discriminatory practice for a fire department or company to deny membership in a volunteer fire department or company therein, or to expel or discriminate against a volunteer member because of race, creed, color or national origin. Other relative provisions. (Co-sponsor.)

1968 Session
Mrs. Chisholm introduced or co-sponsored 29 bills.

United States Congresswoman Shirley Chisholm

91st Congress, 1969-1970
Mrs. Chisholm introduced or co-sponsored 167 bills; of these the following was passed:

> Public Law 91-277, a joint resolution extending for four years the existing authority for the erection in the District of Columbia of a memorial to Mary McLeod Bethune. (Co-sponsor.)

92nd Congress, 1971-1972
Mrs. Chisholm introduced or co-sponsored 98 bills.

93rd Congress, 1973-1974.
Mrs. Chisholm introduced or co-sponsored 478 bills.

BIBLIOGRAPHY

Books and Articles

Brownmiller, Susan. "This is Fighting Shirley Chisholm." *The New York Times Magazine* (April 13, 1969), pp. 32-33ff.

Chisholm, Shirley. *The Good Fight*. New York: Harper & Row, Inc., 1973.

————. *Unbought and Unbossed*. Boston: Houghton Mifflin Company, 1970.

Haskins, James. *Adam Clayton Powell: Portrait of a Marching Black*. New York: The Dial Press, Inc., 1974.

————. Profiles in Black Power. New York: Doubleday and Co., Inc., 1972.

Lesher, Stephen. "The Short, Unhappy Life of Black Presidential Politics, 1972," *The New York Times Magazine* (June 25, 1972), pp. 12-13ff.

Osofsky, Gilbert. *Harlem: The Making of a Ghetto*. New York: Harper Torchbooks, 1968.

Speeches Delivered by Shirley Chisholm

"A Congresswoman Looks at the Urban Crisis," delivered to the American Academy of Psychoanalysis, December 5, 1971.

"And God Reigneth… " (undated)

"The Black Family" (undated)

"Black Politics and Black Politicians," copyright 1970.

"The Busing Dilemma" (undated)

"The Church's Role in the Black Revolution (undated)

"Community Health and Community Participation," presented at the 1970 Health Conference of the New York Academy of Medicine, April 23, 1970.

"The Current Thrust in Higher Education," delivered before the Iowa University Student Body, March 2, 1973.

"Equal Rights, A Bill Long Overdue," delivered in the U.S. House of Representatives, October 6, 1971.

"Faith is Not Enough—Commitment is Needed," delivered at the Congressional Prayer Breakfast, U.S. Capitol, September 14, 1972.

"The 51 Percent Minority," delivered at the Conference on Women's
    Employment, January 1970.

"The Food Stamp Issue" (undated)

"Ghetto Power in Action: The Value of Positive Political Action" (undated)

"How Christian Women Can Meet the Challenge of the New Revolution,"
    delivered at the New Bethel Baptist Church, Washington, D.C.,
    October 22, 1972.

"Of Course Women Dare" (undated)

"Political Concerns of Women," delivered at the Annual Convention of the
    National Association of Women Deans and Counselors, New York City,
    New York, March 24, 1972.

"Progress Through Understanding," Howard University Commencement
    Address, June 6, 1969.

"Race Relations and Tensions in America Today" (undated)

"The Role of an Activist in Supporting Consumer Interests," delivered before
    the Association of Home Appliance Manufacturers, Boston,
    Massachusetts, December 1, 1972.

"The Search for a Quality Life," delivered to the American Health Congress,
    Chicago, Illinois, August 10, 1972.

Speech (untitled) delivered to the National Women's Political Caucus,
    Houston, Texas, February 9, 1973.

Statement on Abortion before the Republican Task Force on Earth Resources
    and Population, Washington, D.C., December 3, 1969.

Statement before the Office of Federal Contract Compliance, August 6, 1969.

Statement before the Select Subcommittee on Education of the House
    Committee on Education and Labor on Preschool Education and Day
    Care, March 4, 1970.

Statement to the North Carolina Education Association, Greensboro, April 7,
    1972.

Statement to the House Armed Services Committee, March 11, 1971.

Testimony before the House Select Committee on Crime, September 17,
    1969.

Testimony delivered before the Subcommittee on Constitutional
Amendments of the Senate Judiciary Committee, May 5, 1970.

Testimony before the General Labor Subcommittee of the House Education
and Labor Committee on H.R. 1746, The Equal Employment
Opportunities Enforcement Act, March 18, 1971.

Testimony before the House Judicary Committee on H.R. 916, Presidential
Task Force on Women's Rights, March 24, 1971.

Testimony before the Select Subcommittee on Education of the House
Committee on Education and Labor on the Need for a National Day Care
Program, May 17, 1971.

Testimony prepared for delivery before the Senate Subcommittee on
Employment, Manpower, and Poverty, March 19, 1970.

"The Urban Crisis" (undated)

"Welfare Reform or Enforced Poverty," delivered before the National Welfare
Rights Organization's Third Biennial Convention, Providence,
Rhode Island, July 31, 1971.

INDEX

ABM (antiballistic missile), 124
Abortion issue, 127-129, 134, 159
Afro-American Teachers Association, 133
Agnew, Spiro T., 113
Anthony, Susan B., 127-128, 134, 159
Antipoverty programs, 161
Antiwar movement, 123, 126
Barbadians, in New York, 11, 12
Bedford-Stuyvesant Political League, 38, 42,
   48, 50, 61, 73, 74, 77, 82, 91, 95, 100-
   101, 104, 107, 133
Bethune, Mary McLeod, 51
Black Muslims, 80, 98
Blacks: and abortion issue, 127-129, 133,
   159; history, 32-33; immigration from
   West Indies, 11, 33; migration to North,
   11; at 1972 Democratic National Con-
   vention, 154; in politics, 63; representa-
   tion in Congress, 63, 122. See also Civil
   Rights Movement
Boggs, Halek, 132
Bond, Julian, 137-138, 142
Brooklyn Local Economic Development
   Center, 133
Buchanan, Bessie, 89-90
Busing, 146, 149, 172
California primary of 1972, 153
Charles Drew Neighborhood Health Center,
   133
Cheetah Charter Bus Service Company, 133
Chisholm, Conrad, 70-11, 76-79, 83-88, 91,
   96-97 102-103, 106, 110-114, 188, 130,
   132, 138, 141, 144, 153-154, 166-167
Chisholm, Shirley: birth, 13; campaign
   for Congress, 101-116; charged with
   misuse of campaign funds, 165-168;
   college education, 53-66; college
   extracurricular activities, 58-64; Congresswoman, 117-129, 147; Democratic National Committee- woman, N.Y.
   112-113, 131; early years on Barbados,
   17-26; education, 19-21, 24, 30-32, 39,
   42-49; in local Brooklyn politics, 60-62,

71-80, 76-79, 81-88; marriage, 70-71;
   N.Y. Assemblywomen, 85-101; on N.Y.
   Assembly Committee on Education,
   93-94, 100; postgraduate work, 67;
   Presidential candidate, 138-159; reli-
   gion, 22-23, 36-38; teaching career, 66,
   74-77, 78-80
Civil Rights Movement, 79-81, 106-107
Clay, William, 154
Congress, U.S., 117-134; committee as-
   signments, 119-120; committees, see
   House Agriculture Committee, etc.;
   seniority system, 120,125, 132-133,
   147-148, 163-164
Congress of Racial Equality (CORE), 80, 109
Consumer Action Program,
   Bedford-Stuyvesant, 133
Day-care services, 78-79, 133, 149
Defense spending bills, 123-124, 131-132
Democratic National Convention of 1968,
   112-113, 154
Democratic National Convention of 1972,
   135-159; candidates, 136; delegates,
   136-137, 142-143, 148-159; delega-
   tion challenges, 156-157; minority
   representation, 137, 141-142, 151, 156;
   platform, 149; rules challenges, 156-
   157; votes for Chisholm, 157-158; votes
   for McGovern, 153-154, 157-158
Department of Defense, U.S., 123
Depression of 1930s, 24, 33-35
Desegregation, 80. See also Busing; Inte-
   gration
District offices, congressional, 125-126,
   133-134
Domestic workers, 94; and minimum wage
   coverage, 162-163
Du Bois, W.E.B., 49, 51, 56
Eagleton, Thomas, 159
Education bills, N.Y. State, 93, 100
Employment, 125, 133
Evers, Charles, 7, 158
Farmer, James, 109-115
Fauntroy, Walter, 126, 147, 154, 156
Flagg, Lewis, 73-77
Florida primary of 1972, 144-147

Food programs, 161
Fortune, Thomas, 113
Freedom Rides, 80, 109
Friend in Need Nursery, N.Y., 75
Galamison, Milton, 102
Garrett, Thaddeus, 139
Garvey, Marcus, 33-34, 47, 50, 81
General Accounting Office (GAO), 166-167
Gerrymandering, 97
Ghettos, 100, 161
Golar, Simeon, 87
Goring, Ruth, 83-84
Hamilton-Madison House Child Care Center,
    N.Y., 75-76, 79
Head Start, 124
Holder, Wesley McD., 61-62, 73-74, 77-
    79,104, 112, 125, 138
House Agriculture Committee, 120-122
House Education and Labor Committee,
    120, 131-132, 145, 148, 161, 164
House Veterans' Affairs Committee, 123, 148
House Ways and Means Committee, 121
Housing, 93, 114, 124, 126, 133
Humphrey, Hubert H., 113, 136-137, 141,
    146, 151, 153
Immigration from West Indies, 11, 33
Integration. See also Busing, 80, 82
Jews, 12, 102, 108
Job procurement and training, 125-126, 133
Jones, Thomas R., 82-86, 91
Kennedy, John F., 107-108, 152
Kennedy, Robert F., 107-108, 152
King, Martin Luther, Jr., 80-82; assassination
    of, 107
King's County Democratic Committee, 102
Legislative redistricting, 96-99, 101-102
Lewis, Charles, 87
Lindsay, John V., 129-131, 134, 137, 140-141,
    147
Malcolm X, 80-82, 91, 97-99; assassination
    of, 99
Marshall, Thurgood, 106
McCormack, John, 118, 120-122
McGovern, George, 136-137, 141, 146,
    153-159
Michigan primary of 1972, 151-152

Mills, Wilbur, 120-121
Minimum Wage Bill of 1973, 165
Mt. Calvary Child Care Center, N.Y., 66, 71, 76
Muskie, Edmund S., 113, 136-137, 146
NAACP, 51, 62, 64, 96, 102, 106
Nation of Islam, 80, 98
National Association for the Repeal of Abor-
    tion Laws, 127-129, 133, 159
National Black Political Convention, 1972,
    154
New York City: Division of Day Care, 78-79;
    political clubs, 60, 82; West Indian
    immigrants, 19-20
New York State: aid to education, 93-94, 101;
    12th Congressional District of, 102-103,
    108, 126
New York State Assembly, 87, 89-101; 55th
    District, 104-106
Nixon, Richard M., 113, 116, 124, 136, 162
Nixon Administration, 165-166
Nostrand Democratic Club, Brooklyn, 82
Office of Economic Opportunity (OEO),
    161-162
One man, one vote decision, 101
Powell, Adam Clayton, Jr., 7, 50-51, 63, 74,
    95, 101, 106, 122-123, 132, 164, 167
Primary elections, 1972, 136, 144-148,
    150-155
Procaccino, Mario, 129-131
Puerto Ricans, 76, 84, 100, 120
Racism, 57, 107, 144
Redistricting, 97, 99
Richardson, Maude B., 87
Robinson, Dolly, 102, 104, 108
Robinson, Gerald, 145
Rockefeller, Nelson, 95
Rowe, Joseph K., 82-83
St. Hill, Charles, 12-16, 24, 31-36, 39, 44, 47-
    48, 63-64; death of, 85
St. Hill, Muriel, 13, 15, 17, 26-27, 37, 40
St. Hill, Odessa, 13, 26-27, 36-37, 40, 48
St. Hill, Ruby, 12-13, 15-19, 24-27, 32, 36,
    38-39, 41, 47-48, 51-52, 54, 57, 64-65,
    70-71, 73
St. Hill, Selma, 25-26, 28, 37, 40-41
Schools, state aid to, 93

Seale, Emily, 12, 15, 17, 19, 22-23, 26-27, 55, 76
SEEK (Search for Education, Elevation & Knowledge), 100
Segregation, 80, 107, 146
Separatism, Black, 80, 98
17th Assembly District Club, Brooklyn, 61, 67, 69, 71-73, 78-79, 84, 92, 99
Shaw, Fred F., 99
Slavery, 43-45, 49
Smith, Margaret Chase, 144
Southern Christian Leadership Conference (SCLC), 80
Steingut, Stanley, 91, 93
Stokes, Louis, 154, 156
Student activists, in 1972 elections, 135, 138-139, 142, 155, 160
Student Nonviolent Coordinating Committee, 80, 107
Sutton, Percy, 158
Tax reform, 149
Thompson, William C., 102-104, 106, 108
Travia, Anthony, 91-93
Tubman, Harriet, 43-47, 56, 58, 60, 62
Unemployment insurance, 94
Unity Democratic Club, Brooklyn, 82-86, 88, 104
Vann, Jesse L., 99
Vietnam War, 4, 8, 113, 123, 132, 143
Waggoner, Joe D., 132
Wallace, George, 146, 149, 152
Warsoff, Louis, 58-60, 63
Washington, D.C.: Chisholm's help to residents, 126, 133; 1972 primary, 154
Welfare, 111, 133, 149
West Indies, 11, 33
Westchester County (N.Y.) Democratic Committee, 131
Women: and minimum wage bill, 163; at 1972 Democratic National Convention, 138-139, 142, 145, 149, 155-156, 158-159
Women's Liberation, 126-128, 155
World War II, 63